WHAT OTHERS SAY ABC ‖‖ ‖‖ ‖‖‖‖‖ ‖‖ ‖‖‖‖ ‖ ‖‖
"BROKEN ROADS TO GRA   D1246446

This book is "SQUIRREL STEW for the SOUL" − more substantial than chicken soup; you have to chew on it before you swallow it; a little strange-tasting, but you will never forget that you ate it and that it was GOOD!
- Teth Burns, founder and editor of "This That and the Other" magazine

These stories will make you laugh, cry, and even shout for joy as you embrace the message of God's love and the freedom it brings. I appreciate the refreshing authenticity, which is reminiscent of Donald Miller and Jim Palmer.
- Stephen Akinduro, author of "Keeping the Good in the Good News"

Jim Lee gets the radical nature of God's grace as well as anybody I know, and he has a great gift with words... words that often stand up and sing The Hallelujah Chorus!
- Steve Brown, professor of preaching at Reformed Seminary, author, and director of Key Life ministries, Orlando Florida

"Broken Roads to Grace" is a delightful tour through God's fields of mercy. Your tour guide is Jim Lee, a "formerly fundamentalist preacher" who spent years in the "performance trap" before being found by grace. This book is literally overflowing with dramatic experiences that reveal the good news of God's radical love.
- Claire Cloninger, award-winning Christian author and songwriter

Open to any story in this book, and you will find your mind will be captivated by it! Broken Roads to Grace is a raw, real look at the authentic journey of Jim Lee. It doesn't come across as pious or religious, but it is deeply spiritual and thoughtful. You will laugh, cry, and maybe even get mad as you explore your own journey of grace through broken roads. You owe it to yourself to read it with an open heart and allow grace to amaze you once again!

- Richard Mark Lee, lead pastor of First Baptist Church, McKinney, Texas

In this book, Jim Lee has wonderfully captured and beautifully explained some of the most meaningful, refreshing and insightful examples of God's radical grace. It explodes the myths that God is distant or harsh.

- Bill Purvis, lead pastor of Cascade Hills Church, Columbus, Georgia

Jim Lee is a storyteller, and a "recovering" preacher. Some of his stories are funny, some are simple yet insightful observations, and still others are the interesting or edifying recountings of events in people's lives. It is deeper spiritual truth put in words that are easy to understand, profusely illustrated by life's experiences. All of these stories magnify the freedom, healing, and restoration that only grace can bring... grace that continues to heal his heart, and mine. I commend my friend to you... hear and receive this grace writer as you walk or even as you stumble on the broken roads of life.

- Reverend Mark DiCristina, Associate Minister, Church of the Apostles, Fairhope, Alabama

IF YOU REALLY LIKE THIS BOOK, and...

If you would you like more copies of "Broken Roads to Grace" ...

Or if you would like to order the two-CD audio book of "Broken Roads to Grace"...

Or if you want to order several copies at a discounted price...

Or if you want to follow Jim Lee's weekly blog...

Or if you want info on Jim Lee's next book ...

Then please go online to:
www.brokenroadstograce.com

Email Jim Lee at:
jim@brokenroadstograce.com

Or order by mail from:

P U B L I S H I N G
7166 SHARP REEF
PERDIDO KEY, FL 32507

BROKEN ROADS
to GRACE

Jim Lee

Lost Key
PUBLISHING
PENSACOLA, FL

Broken Roads to Grace

Copyright 2011 by Jim Lee
International Standard Book Number: 978-0-9823946-2-5

Published by:

PUBLISHING

7166 Sharp Reef Road
Pensacola, FL 32507

Foreword

The weather was cool and crisp. I was alone in a small remote cabin, accompanied only by my twelve-year-old mixed breed dog that I had named Statler because I liked the Statler Brothers quartet.

I had been awakened just before dawn by the sound of a rooster crowing somewhere in the distance. I staggered into the kitchen, fumbled with the coffee pot, and started the coffee, making it extra strong as I always do. I sat down in my favorite chair and wished to go back to sleep, but by now the sun was beginning to come up.

Back in the kitchen, I fixed something for Statler and then warmed up a big bowl of leftover grits and fried two eggs and one slice of bacon. Within five minutes it was all ready, and in five more minutes I had finished it, cleared the table, and put the dishes in the sink. I poured myself a second cup of coffee and sat down with it at the long, rustic table overlooking the woods.

About fifteen minutes later, while I still was finishing my coffee, I looked over and saw a young man walking up the steps to my front porch. I had not noticed a vehicle in my driveway, so, for all I knew, he may have walked to my place. He knocked on my front door and waited. Strangely, Statler didn't even bark but just stood there watching the door and wagging his tail.

I knew the man, had seen him a few times before, but certainly did not know him very well. I opened the door and let him in and poured him a cup of coffee, which he took with a smile. We sat together at the table with our cups of coffee. He was only about half my age, with dark tanned skin, simple sandals on his feet, and a face that looked as if he had borne a lot of sorrow and pain, yet his eyes seemed to have an intense joyfulness, and his smile was genuine.

With a soft voice, he began to speak. He didn't give me any information or instructions or advice. He didn't explain to me what he was doing, or why he was here at my table.

He only did one thing. He told me some stories.

$$\approx$$

Chapter five, chapter ten, and the little story here are not literally, physically true. They are clearly fantasies, and are labelled as such. All of the other events actually happened and are unforgettable in my life.

I was taught to preach and teach with the idea of stating my point at the beginning, giving the Scripture reference, and then giving it the support that was needed to reinforce whatever had already been said. What a boring teaching method!

Jesus did it a better way. He told things in story form, without giving away the punch line. He took us with him on a journey that ended up in a profound realization of personal truth. You could never predict what he was going to say.

Now it goes without saying that I am no Jesus, but I would be crazy to not try to learn from his methods and his example. Therefore, whatever "expository exegesis" knowledge that I may have has been put away on a shelf somewhere gathering more dust. "Broken Roads to Grace" is mostly a book of stories for all of us "common" people.

I am writing it for men and women who want to consider themselves as Christians and want a relationship with God, but, to be honest, there are some obstacles in their way. Perhaps they have been wounded by religion or religious people. Maybe they just don't think that they are good enough. They might be afraid they will be criticized, rejected, manipulated, condemned, or confused. It could be that preachers and sermons and church stuff just makes them angry, or worse than that... it just puts them to sleep.

If any of this describes you, then you are my "target audience!" Have a good time with it, and listen for "the soft sound of sandaled feet."

Broken Roads to Grace

Contents

Preface

by Steve Brown

I teach communications at a theological seminary, and, as a part of that job, I teach lab classes where students have an opportunity to preach before the class and to hear the comments of the other students and of course, my own comments.

There are a number of ways by which I measure a good sermon, but one of the main ways I judge a sermon is by how often I say, "I don't believe I would have said that," to wit, the more I say it, the better the sermon. That's important because it is always better for a preacher to shock people than to bore them.

If the Christian faith isn't shocking, amazing, liberating, disturbing, and fun, then it's probably not the Christian faith.

You hold in your hands a book that will cause you to say often, "I don't believe I would have said that." You'll say that because Jim Lee gets the radical nature of God's grace as well as anybody I know. Not only that, but he has a great gift with words — words that often stand up and sing The Hallelujah Chorus! He writes with great power and insight, and this book will make you laugh, cry, think, and even get angry. But you'll think in a different way about God and about life.

Jim Lee took his "mask" off a long time ago, and his authenticity will sometimes stun you. There is wisdom here, and love and power. And it all rests on truth — the truth that changes lives.

I hope that a lot of people will read this book. They will become more free and more genuine if they do.

Read "Broken Roads to Grace" by Jim Lee, and you will, along with me, rise up and "call him blessed!"

Introduction

Well...Hi!

I didn't know whether I would find you over here or not! Personally, when I am reading a book, I usually skip the introduction and go straight to chapter one, where the "real action" can be found. You, being one who does read introductions, know how dumb that is.

I even thought about skipping the writing of the introduction, but now that you are here, that would not be a very nice thing for me to do. It could leave you staring at a blank page! So I owe you at least this much. Just for you, I will attempt to make this a fantastic introduction.

"Broken Roads to Grace" is a book of forty-eight short chapters from a formerly fundamentalist preacher who spent most of his "ministry" thinking that he had to get it right and to be right and to live right beyond all reasonable human expectations. It was essentially that awful religious thing known as a "performance trap." The horrible thing about basing everything on your own performance (whether faithfulness or obedience or service) is that whether you do it right or not, you lose. When you don't perform well, you get discouraged.

Then when you do perform well, you become proud, which is even worse.

But most of this book doesn't dwell on that. Instead, these chapters will tell my experiences of being found by grace, as well as my reflections and insights on life as I have come to understand it now.

I am trying to come from a viewpoint of honesty. The real me, with all of my flaws and messed-up ways, is the only "me" that really exists. Even God (especially God) cannot have a relationship with an illusion, an image, or a false self. Like everyone, I want to be liked, approved, accepted, and appreciated, and I'm afraid that I won't get that from you if you really know me. But the only thing harder than being honest is trying to live with yourself when you aren't.

In "Blue Like Jazz," Donald Miller wrote "There is not a lot of work in the Christian market if you won't write self-righteous, conservative propaganda. I write new-realism essays. I am not a commodity." Wow! Don, you are my hero! So I guess you could call "Broken Roads" kind of a new-realism thing. That means that if you are looking for a neat, safe Christian book, there are plenty of them out there that are perhaps not as candid and thence a better commodity.

For example: Chapter One relates that one of the most effective prayers I ever prayed was full of sarcasm and profanity. Chapter Two says that we will never again experience an "old-fashioned revival." Chapter Three tells of a murder-suicide in my family history. Chapter Four approves of a name for a church that some would find to be tasteless and offensive. Chapter Five seems to be against all kinds of Christian stuff you can buy. Chapter Six leaves you hanging without a satisfying conclusion. Chapter Seven reveals my absurd heritage of racism. And so it goes throughout the book.

I am basically a speaker/broadcaster rather than a literary scholar. I "write for the ear." Practically everything that I have put on paper since seminary has been written to be read aloud (sermons, radio talks, commercials, classroom lectures and such.) That is my reason (okay, my excuse) for phrasing things in a different way than a scholar would. (A scholar would write "than would a scholar." People read that way, but they don't talk that way!)

Most of these chapters are in the form of true stories which come from my childhood, from school, or from many varied experiences as a pastor and a radio broadcaster. I also have spent some time as a college professor, a truck driver, a car salesman, and a traveling bass singer in a quartet. So don't be surprised if some of these writings are as weird as I am. Nevertheless I am seriously involved in thinking about what these stories really have to say and what meaning they can have to myself and to others.

Now here's some good news: if you have read this far, I believe that you will like this book! I am pretty certain that some Christians perhaps would not like it, but most of them have already stopped reading it by now. So I hope that you will give it a chance, take the risk, and think about some of the opinions and interpretations that I am trying to share. I believe that Christians should not be afraid to think, or to doubt, or to change. Sure, I push the envelope sometimes, but those who know me would reassure you that I am not a heretic. I just put a different spin on some things.

None of this stuff comes from a cold observer in an ivory tower. (Do people really say that any more?) Admittedly they come from some sort of preacher… but not a sinless one, not one who has it all together and isn't acquainted with his own propensities to throw the train off the track. I know the meaning of most curse words, am well acquainted with lust, and usually drive just enough over the speed limit so that I won't get a ticket. I have been spotted going through the drive-thru window at Chick-fil-A between meals. Be assured I am leaving some stuff out that would blow your mind, just as your unedited story would short-circuit mine. I have stumbled more times than I can keep track of. I know how to offend lots of people and mess things up royally for everybody. Sometimes I can get a lot of this done before breakfast and still have most of the day left over.

Normally I don't use a lot of religious-sounding language. I have noticed that even in church most people will get a glazed-over look in their eyes when someone stiffly begins with "Turn with me in your Bibles to chapter nine ..." Therefore I deliberately use simple terms, tell simple stories, avoid religious clichés, and try to be a little more earthy. But the content can still be spiritual. It can even sometimes be deeper than we think.

The heart of this book is really all about grace. In so many different ways, I am trying to show that the grace of God, even with all of its weird and wild implications, is really true. The message was given for sinners, not for "good Christians"... which is why I love it so much.

I am from the South. I know what real biscuits, real grits, and real pit barbecue taste like. Then somebody came along with canned biscuits, instant grits, and barbecue that you can fix in thirty minutes. (Whoever did that, their soul is in danger!) But just like those horrible substitutes, the pre-packaged, quick and easy version of a spiritual life is nothing like the real thing. That's why we call it a "broken road." In this book I will share some of my own experiences of pain and sorrow and failure, and of love and forgiveness and restoration.

These forty-eight little chapters are simply arranged alphabetically. When you read them you may laugh, or you may cry, or you may just roll your eyes and say, "Oh brother!" It's all cool with yours truly. Hey, I'm just glad to have you looking at the page! I have even included a few chapters that are relatively sweet and harmless.

However you may approach these "broken roads to grace," I hope that you will find it to be enlightening, powerful, challenging, spiritual, and profound. But if not, I hope at least that it will be fun.

Even that will be enough for me.

Jim Lee

1

A Desperate,
Non-Religious Prayer

"Praise and thanksgiving really is not for the benefit of God at all. God is strong and secure, and He doesn't need it. Praise and giving of thanks is for us!"

It was the summer of 2000, and I was going through one of the worst times of my entire life. I was devastated over something that was just breaking my heart and was beyond my control to change. Compounding the misery of the situation was the knowledge that much of what had happened was my fault. We are not always gracious to ourselves, and when we aren't it adds guilt and shame to what is already a terrible problem.

We've all been through some hurts and disappointments, but this was more than that. "Devastation" is probably the best word for it, because my world as I knew it seemed to be coming to an end; and as T.S. Eliot described it, it was "not with a bang, but a whimper." Regret and remorse and a sickening sadness were my closest companions. I was convinced that I was deserving of this great loss, yet the loss was so great that I did not want to go on. If you've ever been there, you know what I am trying to say. If you haven't, no words can describe it to you anyhow.

I was sitting in the swing on my back porch overlooking the woods on a Saturday morning. The birds were singing, but my heart had no song. I had cried all the tears I could cry, and I had begged, pleaded, and literally screamed to no avail. I had been unsuccessful in my attempts to manipulate God, promising that I would "do anything if only..." and had gone through phases of denial, anger, self-pity, bargaining, and all the other steps of handling grief, and it seemed that I was just getting worse. I had settled into a deep hopelessness. I was at the proverbial "end of my rope." If the rope hadn't been proverbial I think I would have tied it around my neck.

On that occasion, as dark as it was, something special happened to me that Saturday.

It started with what I suppose you could call a prayer, although it was not a religious prayer. It would not make the list of any great prayers that I have ever heard. I have prayed fancy prayers before, often in church. I have prayed some prayers that sounded so spiritual they could have elevated me to sainthood! How effective they were is questionable.

But this simple prayer was nothing that would impress them in church. The prayer was short but not sweet. It went like this:

"Okay, God, what in *#%*@># am I supposed to do now?"

It is so remarkable that God seems to ignore some of the great lofty prayers, yet would take the time to give an immediate response to a desperate, non-religious prayer. This prayer, if you would call it a prayer at all, was more profane than profound. Of course, I didn't really expect an answer.

But then, very distinctly, there was a clear, unmistakable voice whispering softly to my angry, bitter, destroyed heart.

The voice simply said, "You can be thankful."

"Thankful?" I blurted out, before I realized how unusual it was to have heard such a clear message. "You have got to be kidding! What kind of cruel joke is this to me? What do I have to be thankful for?"

There was no other reply. I knew, of course that God was not going to get into an argument with me.

(I do not hear God talking to me all the time. I am very suspicious of anybody who says that they have two-way conversations with the Lord. He has never told me what groceries to buy or what soap to use. I am also suspicious of evangelists who advertise "miracles and healings" in their meetings, as if He does it "on cue!" Not meaning to hurt your ministry, brothers, but the workings of a sovereign God, and the hearing of His voice, are not so predictable that you can put it into your schedule.)

So anyway, having heard what I heard, and still feeling very hurt and bitter, I sarcastically began to verbally express "thankfulness." It went something like this:

"Okay, God, there's a stupid bird in the tree, chirping away. Thank you for that stupid bird!" (Nothing but silence as my sarcasm filled the air.)

"Okay, this is great. Thank you for the stupid tree that the stupid bird is sitting in."

"So far so good," I may have thought. No great miracle here, but I might actually be feeling about one percent better.

"Okay, thank you that I have eyes to see that stupid bird,

and ears to hear its stupid song! Is that better?"

It continued on like that for some time. My "thankfulness" now was maybe ninety percent sarcastic and ten percent sincere. Then eighty percent sarcastic and twenty percent sincere. After several more minutes I might have been at fifty-fifty. But each expression of thankfulness, as it increased in sincerity, came out a little easier.

"Thank you for my hand that I can use to point at that bird."

"Thank you that I still have five fingers on each hand."

"Thank you for my mind, so that I can know that it is a bird, and a tree, and a hand..."

It had not taken very long. It was still morning. I was still hurting badly, but now I was saying "Thank you for the swing, and the porch, and the door, and for my feet, and for the sweet old dog that came to see me! And thank you, Lord, that you haven't changed... you haven't been surprised by any of this... you are still in control... and you still love me more than I could imagine, and far more than I could ever deserve. Oh Lord, you really have been good to me in lots of ways! It really hurts right now, God... but I surrender it all to you, and I just want to thank you!"

It's hard to imagine how it happened, but this practice of simply saying the words of thanks, even when I didn't mean them, eventually resulted in a drastic change in my heart. The same hands that had been clenched into fists of defiance were now being lifted up in praise, and the same voice that had uttered complaint and cursing was now extolling the glory and greatness of the Lord!

It was then that I learned that praise and thanksgiving really is not for the benefit of God at all. God is strong and secure, and He doesn't need it. Praise and giving of thanks is for us! It gives us strength in the midst of suffering, puts everything in a positive context, and dramatically transforms our attitude. It did it for me on the porch that Saturday, during the most awful time of my life.

The bad times indeed are painful, and some of them are horrible. I am not discounting that. I still cried an awful lot. Sometimes in thinking about it, I still do. It took months before the circumstances changed.

We should never flippantly tell a person who is really devastated to "just cheer up and praise the Lord." That's a good way to get your arm broken! Spare the poetry and clichés and quick fixes and Bible verses. Just as I did, people have to work through it a little at a time.

But when you really think that you can't go on any more, please remember that He is there. He knows all about it. And He cares enough to bring you through in one piece, even better than you were.

No matter how bad it may be, you can be thankful for a lot of things. I have it on the highest authority.

You may start with the nearest little bird.

2

A Final Call to Change Things

"Following the way of Christ is not exactly the same thing as protecting and defending our particular flavor of Christianity."

I remember it well, even though it actually was many years ago. Our family was going through a hard time, so I thought that it would help and encourage us if we visited a midweek prayer meeting church service.

Unfortunately, I was wrong. The prayer time was mostly a boring mixture of gossip and discouragement. The rest of the time was spent discussing the plans for a new building. We left feeling angry and disappointed, as if we had gone to a fish fry and they were out of fish.

However, this turned out to be the wake-up call that I

needed, as I realized that this same kind of thing was happening to many people everywhere in this country. They walk in, they find nothing that relates to them, they walk out, and they never come back. Yet, even today, across this land there are pockets of faithful people who are still trying to hang on to the way they did it fifty years ago. They are dismayed over the fact that not as many people come out to the services any more. This bothers them so much because in their minds they consider that faithfulness to attend all the services is the same as faithfulness to Christ. So they think that people just don't want God in their lives any more, that we are living in a hopelessly evil world, and that what we need is a "revival."

I would like to propose an alternate interpretation, if I may.

I think that there are a lot of people who *do* want God in their lives, but we will never have an "old-fashioned revival" because the old ways of doing religion no longer communicate with most people. During our lifetime, our culture, including the way people think, has changed.

The problem is that somewhere along the way we took the Gospel message and mixed it up with our own nostalgia for the "good old days" of the brush-arbor meetings, the fire-and-brimstone preachers, and the come-to-church mentality. Now we don't know how to separate the two.

But separate the two we must!

The Gospel was not meant to be locked in a time-warp the way Grandma used to do it! Thank God for all the things He used in the past, but if we want people to listen today, we must be willing to change the way we tell the story.

We must tell it with our lives, our attitudes, and our practical service to others.

We must throw away old churchy-sounding words that nobody uses any more.

We must stop judging people, pressuring people, and manipulating people through guilt and shame.

We must not be afraid to use "worldly" things such as movies and secular songs because God is well able to speak His truth through all of these things.

If we are serious about reaching the people who inhabit the culture of today and tomorrow, then our songs, our presentation, our vocabulary, and our methods must undergo a major alteration.

Furthermore, some of our rigid theology needs to be bathed in a new openness, a new compassion, a new humility of mind. We must come to realize that God wants to do so much more with us than to just give us a "personal" salvation or be a "personal savior" just for us to be ready to go to Heaven when we die or to avoid being "left behind" when He comes back.

He has entrusted us with making this world a better place where the love of God can heal relationships and transform lives. "May your kingdom come, and your will be done, as it is in Heaven, so on earth!"

Once we come outside of the strict legalistic traditional tent, we will be able to breathe lots and lots of fresh air! We will see that the Kingdom of God is not contained within the walls nor the established statements of the church.

We will see that following the way of Christ is not exactly the same thing as protecting and defending our particular flavor of Christianity.

We will allow for others to disagree with us on many

things and still be considered as brothers.

We will learn from others and not put labels on them.

And we will begin to help some hurting people without first making sure they endorse our theology or pray the prayers that we want them to pray.

We've got to learn to picture Jesus with his arms wide open, not folded in a rejecting posture. Then, we must show ourselves to have that same openness to others.

We will do so much better if we can turn our evangelism around backward. For years, we have told people to believe, and then they can belong. Now, I strongly feel that we must first make sure that people know that they are genuinely accepted as they are, and that they belong with us. Then they will be likely to stay around and, suddenly or gradually, they will begin to believe.

Quite a few years back Bill Gaither wrote a song with a very long and strange title. It was called, "Don't Want to Spend My Time Writing Songs That Answer Questions That Nobody's Even Asking Anyhow!" It was indeed a good song.

The message of Christ, in order to powerfully relate to people's lives today, must be presented by people who are humbly authentic, ready to listen to others, and open to new ideas and ways. If we aren't... well, our audience has already shrunk and will someday soon be gone.

There are, of course, some who refuse to see this and will never change. I recently had to stop broadcasting on an "old time religion" radio station because my program was described as "too secular and too entertaining!" In my communicating with the audience, I dared to refer to worldly events and non-religious songs and movies rather than bore people with worn-out Christian clichés.

But I think that the ostriches are running out of sand.

The fact that there is still so much hunger and homelessness and racism, neglect and abuse and needless suffering is an indictment upon our "just-be-saved-and-be-ready-to-die" theology. Jim Palmer relates in "Divine Nobodies," that upon discovering that nine- and ten-year-old girls were being sold as sex-slaves in Thailand, he asked God, "How could you let this happen?" And God said back to him, "How could *you* let this happen?" The point is that we have been given resources to change things, and instead we have built religious systems that are now falling down in a heap of irrelevance.

I am ready to make a shocking recommendation for your consideration. Next week, instead of going to a midweek prayer meeting, get a friend to go with you to a coffee shop or even a bar, and just "hang out" and listen to people's stories. Show them that you care enough to really listen. Don't be in a hurry to change them or fix them... just show the love of Christ through your life and your attitude. It won't be long before they ask you questions, and then you can tell them about your experiences of forgiveness and divine power in your life.

If your story is real, God will speak to them without pressure from you.

Oh, and before you go, ask the good church folks, when they meet together, to also pray for you as you "hit the bars!" Tell them that you are going to report back, and that they are invited, whenever they are ready, to go with you.

That will probably wake up their meeting, too!

3

A Hero of Mine

"Every time I see an old Dodge automobile... every time I walk into a small hometown grocery store...and many times when I stop and think of what is the 'right' thing to do in my life, I think of her."

She was a survivor if I ever met one. I'm so glad that I got to know her well. Just yesterday I took a look at her picture again — a picture probably taken in the mid-fifties. Here is her story:

She was the wife of a man who ran a sawmill and the mother of six children, not counting one that had been stillborn. In the midst of rearing these six children in a family in a small town, her husband had an affair with another woman. The other woman decided that she was going to tell his family, so he went to her place and fatally shot her. Then he came home, wrote a note of apology for what he had done, and, on a beautiful Sunday afternoon, he used the same gun on himself. Some of the girls heard the shot, and one of them ran out into the grove behind their house and found her father lying dead.

The news was everywhere by the next morning. As people sometimes do, the neighbors chose to gossip about the situation and about the family. "Of course," they "felt sorry" for what this lady was going through, losing her husband so tragically. But the family was now "shamed."

This was during the Great Depression of the early thirties. The stock market had crashed, people were out of work, and this "shamed" family now had no income. Within a matter of a few weeks, there was not much money, there were very few friends and very few possessions left.

I don't know how long she stayed in that little town, but I don't think that it was very long before she took her six children, moved to a larger city, and for five hundred dollars bought a little twenty-foot square wooden building that had been a barbecue shack. She then contacted a wholesale grocery company and opened up the "Lula Olive Grocery Store" in that little building.

Keeping the store open from six until six every day but Sunday, without any other employees, she made enough to support the family and to buy a house. Eventually, she bought another house on the same street. She also somehow found the time to train her children to "live right, work hard, have fun, and be nice to people." (I still think those are four good rules to live by.) She set the example and made very sure that all six of them followed it, which they did for their entire lives. She never re-married.

Thirty years later, she had finally retired and stayed busy helping her children and grandchildren. It was 1963, and I was in college studying for the ministry.

One Saturday morning I decided to go to see her. I drove

my 1951 Dodge Coronet (which she had sold to me at a great price) out to her house for a pleasant visit. We talked about a lot of things, laughed a lot, and had ham sandwiches together for lunch. I remember that just before I left she asked me, "What does the Bible say about the possibility of one who has committed suicide going to heaven?"

She didn't know it, but I'm sure that I knew why she had asked me that question. She had never stopped loving her husband, and she was hoping he had gone to a happy place.

My answer seemed to give her comfort. I drove away glad that I had taken this time to be with her.

The following Tuesday she started feeling ill and tired, but she still kept going through most of the day. In the afternoon she sat down in a chair, asked for a glass of water, and quietly passed away. Her heart had just quit beating. She was seventy-six.

I couldn't cry when she died. I somehow felt that I didn't need to. We had said everything that we needed to say just three days ago.

Of course, it has been many years since 1963, but her memory has stayed with me. Whenever I begin to doubt whether I can make it, whether I can survive the trials of life, whether I can keep on going and loving and giving, I remind myself that Lula Olive's blood runs through my veins.

And I remember what she said: "Live right, work hard, have fun, and be nice to people."

Every time I see an old Dodge automobile... every time I walk into a small hometown grocery store... and many times when I stop and think of what is the "right" thing to do in my life... I think of her.

The man who lay dead in the groves was my grandfather. The girls who heard the shot were my mother and her sisters. Lula Olive was my grandmother.

She, and people like her, need to be remembered for a long time.

And, Mama Olive... you know that I will never forget.

4

A Hollow Respectability

"The grace of God is so much greater than all of our religious qualifications that it nullifies our need to even acknowledge them!"

A popular song by Aretha Franklin says, "All I want is a little respect." If we are honest, we know that it is an understatement. We want more than just a little respect. We want recognition! We want admiration! We want to be the center of attention! Whether we admit it or not, we have all, at times, wanted to be a star.

It is not surprising that thousands of people line up for their audition to be the next "American Idol." It is more than a little comical that many fancy themselves as the winner even though they obviously can't sing.

If we pay some attention to the lessons of life, we learn a little humility along the way. We realize that there are some things we will never have a talent for. We know that, even if we are good at something, there will always be somebody somewhere who can do it better. The boxer Muhammad Ali brashly proclaimed that he was "the greatest." But even if he was for a while, it didn't last very long.

There was once a man who walked on this earth and refused to play this silly game. People really tried hard to get him to go their way, but, though he was human, he seemed to just be made differently.

His teaching turned everything upside down. He said that to be first we must be last. He said that in order to be great we must become the servant of all. He said that what we want to keep we must give away. He said that to be strong we must acknowledge our helplessness and weakness. He even said that to experience life in a new way we must die to the old ways. And he taught that to become righteous we must see ourselves as sinners.

Many of us profess to believe in this man enough to want to follow him, wherever he leads, throughout our lives. But it is a big order to change our whole way of thinking.

This stuff is not only difficult... it is impossible without outside help. Scripture says that we can be "transformed by the renewing of our minds." But somehow we often miss the point of what he taught and the example that he set for us.

Many of us have tried doing things "in His name," but we tried to do those things according to our own selfish ways. Wonder why it never did work very well?

How often have we boasted that we have the largest church, the fastest-growing ministry, the most articulate preacher, the greatest singers, or the finest choir?

How many times have we gloried in raising the most

money or winning the most converts or having the nicest buildings in town?

Why is it that every city has a "first" church of every denomination?

How can we continue to be so blatantly competitive with other followers of this same man?

When have we last considered what *He* might think of all of this?

Who are we really trying to impress? And most importantly, *why*?

Thankfully, some of Christ's followers have finally begun to get the point, but we have a long way to go. Nevertheless, it is a start. Recently, I was gratified to notice that all of the front doors of a local church were marked "servant's entrance." Can you imagine how powerfully different we would be if there were no "big shots" and only servants like He taught us to be?

What would happen if we stopped competing, comparing, and counting? I am not exaggerating when I say that for most of my life the two things we always did in church was count the people and count the money! Sadly, the underlying truth was that we were measuring our success in those terms. We wanted to reassure ourselves that we were "succeeding in God's work." We wanted to be bigger. We wanted to see ourselves as important. We wanted a little respect.

We were completely missing the point.

We are specifically admonished to "judge nothing before the time, until the Lord comes." We are told that there is but one good judge, namely God himself. We are let in on the fact that His thoughts and ways are not the same as ours. Yet, so foolishly, we rush to measure our "success" in terms of numbers and dollars and budgets and bricks.

But, as I said, things are finally beginning to change. Here's an example — an example that may even offend some — but it makes the point well. I was looking at a website called "The Ooze," which always has some interesting articles from a refreshing perspective. To my amazement, I saw a reference to a church in Colorado which is actually called "Scum of the Earth." I found out that there is also a church in Seattle with the same name!

On the "Scum of the Earth" church website, they say that the name is appropriate for two reasons. One, they said, was to let people know that no matter what they have done wrong, they are still wanted and welcomed and loved as they are. They said that they gladly welcome those who are considered to be the scum of the earth.

Secondly, they said that they consider themselves to also be sinners capable of anything, so they include themselves among such scum. They even quoted Scripture references such as I Corinthians 4: 11-13 which says that the early believers were considered as such.

I smiled as I considered what might be the reaction of some people if we said that our church was called by that name!

If I asked you how you would like to be known as a member of a church with such a name, what would you say?

"Hi, Mrs. Peabody, what church do you attend?"

"Oh, my family and I go to 'Scum of the Earth,' sir!"

As for me, I think I really would probably fit pretty well in that place.

Somehow, only by the grace of God, I think I can see it

now. I "get it" that I am not more worthy than anyone else is. I am really not "better" than anybody else, no matter who they are or what they have done.

Well, it is easy to say that but harder to mean it. If you ever met a mean, violent criminal, you might pause before saying it. But then, it is very likely that there were deep wounds from the criminal's upbringing that warped and twisted his personality in ways that I can't imagine or understand. I know that except for God's grace, it could be me. Therefore, I have absolutely no right to look down on anyone.

So I am cool with being called the scum of the earth.

The only reason that I can be cool with such a low evaluation of myself is... that's not the whole story! That's not the final chapter or the ultimate outcome! The good news for all of us "scum of the earth" is that because, for reasons that have nothing to do with any goodness in you or in me, we are wanted... and loved... and forgiven... and accepted... by the One whose opinion really matters.

Once you see the truth of radical grace, you can't un-see it. You don't have to convince anybody that you are "good." You are now free to be really honest, because there's nothing to prove, nothing to protect, nothing to perform, and nothing to pretend.

The grace of God is so much greater than all of our religious qualifications that it nullifies our need to even acknowledge them.

Who cares if we are the biggest or best or first or fastest or greatest? Addressing this subject in Philippians, Paul even described all of his great religious accomplishments as "dung." Of course it is an offensive term! But the prophet Isaiah used a term for our own righteousness that even makes "scum" and "dung" seem mild!

Perhaps we will get the point that what "good people" we are and what "good things" we do are really not that good at all. Who and what we are, if there is anything in us that is "good" at all, is because of something that we didn't earn or pay for or deserve, but was given to us as a gift.

"Amazing grace... saved a wretch like me." But when I stop seeing myself as a wretch, I stop being amazed by grace.

As I look into my own heart, I still struggle with wanting to be respected, acknowledged, and admired. My proud ego continues to be in a battle against amazing grace.

It is a battle I hope to lose.

5

A Parable: Sometimes I Make Myself Sick

"For a moment I thought to myself that I had really done great... but then I heard him say that I had done... nothing."

I was dressed in my nicest suit and driving on the way to church Sunday as I sped past a scruffy old woman walking beside the road. With her was a homely and sad looking little boy. For just a moment I felt something strange, but I was expected to be on time, and I was running a little late.

I do try to go to Sunday school and church regularly, and I sing in the choir, too. I want people to know how much I really love God.

I got me a WWJD bracelet from the Christian gift store, and also a big sticker on my car has the shape of a fish. I'm set to tell the world that I'm a Christian.

Hey, you should see my new Bible! It's got all the great notes in it that help me to understand the doctrines and the original meaning of the Bible words. And I've got lots of other Christian books, too. People will be able to tell that I am a spiritual person. And, I hate to brag, but you should have heard the prayer I prayed in church last week. Everybody was shouting, "Amen!"

To show that I am not ashamed of my faith, I also have several Christian tee shirts. There are magnetic Bible verses on my refrigerator, there is Christian music playing in my car, and (get this!) my license plate says " ILVJSUS." It cost me a little extra to get that put on there, but it's worth the sacrifice to have a chance to witness for my Lord. I'm sure that a lot of people have read that tag and know that I am "a child of the King."

So I was talking to Jesus about all of these great things I had done for him and about the bold stand that I had taken.

It was about then that I noticed that he started to cry. For a moment I thought to myself that I really had done great, and that he was just so overwhelmed and blessed by my devotion to him.

But then I heard him say that I had done... nothing.

His voice seemed to break when he said the word, "nothing."

Stunned, I asked him, "What, then, do you have in mind that I should do?" Immediately I wished that I hadn't asked that question. I was expecting to hear some high-sounding religious inspirational answer. His response turned out to be just the opposite. As best I can explain to you, here is what he had to say:

"There is a man in prison who needs a friend. Visit him and encourage him. He did wrong, but he is so sorry about it,

and so afraid. Many people who think they are better are putting him down now. He must have a friend who will believe in him, so he will not give up.

"There is a family waiting for him and they have no warm clothes. You have plenty. Give them some of your best clothes. Let your children give some of their best clothes to his children.

"There is a man on the street who has no food and no home. He has a name. Learn his name, and look him in the eye and gently call him by name. Then give him food, or take him home with you and let him eat from your table. Do not mention my name until you have done at least that much.

"There is a child who is very sick. Visit her, and see that she gets good medical care. Give her kind words, lots of hugs, and pray with her. Even if you have to sell your tee shirts, your music and your Bible, make sure that she has the medicine that she needs."

"But Lord…" I began to protest.

"That's one more thing. I would rather you not call me 'Lord' until you are ready to do what I say. All of these things that you are so proud of have made a mockery of the whole thing."

I hung my head for several minutes. When I looked up I saw that he was still there. In his eyes, I think I saw a look of hope. He still believed that I could find the way to live a life that wasn't centered on me! And I remembered him saying that whatever I had done unto "the least of these" was what I had done unto him.

Time seemed to pass very slowly the rest of the day. Curling up in a warm recliner, I tried to ponder some of these things.

I asked myself how many times my religion had consisted of fitting into a Christian subculture rather than helping the hurting.

I thought of how we had become a "members only" club where we tried to impress each other and we all knew the language as if it was a special code, but we had little impact on anybody outside the club.

I considered the possibility that our sermons and songs and slogans were just so much "god-talk," and nothing more unless accompanied by some kind of action.

I thought of all the times I had enjoyed a "great service" in church when nobody was really served.

Thinking of my fine home and my fine clothes that I wear when I drive my fine car to my fine church building, something strange occurred to me:

Could it be that the real Jesus I was looking for might better have been found in that scruffy old woman and that sad little boy that I had just driven past?

But I was so "religious" that I missed Him.

Today, finally, I took the first step of genuine faith, obedience, and integrity:

I removed the bumper sticker.

6

A Summer That Still Haunts Me

*"Suddenly, things weren't very funny any more.
Suddenly, nobody was 'cool.'"*

I have included this chapter to remind us of the fact that in
this fallen world in which we live and with our flawed personalities all things do not come to a joyful resolution and a neatly
wrapped conclusion. We carry with us unresolved conflicts, un-
solved problems, and unanswered questions. Not all stories
have a happy ending, at least not in this life. One of the things
we must face if we are to be happy is that we will not always
be happy. Think about it; I'm not trying to be cute. We will be
happier in this life if we let go of the expectation that we
should always be happy! In "The Road Less Traveled" Dr.
Scott Peck put it something like, "Life is difficult, but it will be
less difficult if you know it will be difficult."

When this story was first published in a local magazine it
was the "un-favorite" of all I had written because it had no resolution. But then, a few people (well, two) said it was their fa-

vorite story because it reminded them that life is messy, not so neat and clean as we would like. Reminds me of Alfred Hitchcock's "The Birds." Fade to black and the birds are still there. And so they are. We must deal with it.

So, what I am saying is that this may leave you with something to think about. I hope that it does. I think that most of us are haunted by some memories that can not be fixed with words. One more thing I am trying to do is to take my angst to God. He can handle it. But, like Paul's thorn in the flesh, it still will not be removed. He said that His grace is enough. But I still want it removed. And it hangs right there. A stalemate in a chess match with God.

Enough apologizing for this story! Here it is:

I was so excited to be going to camp one summer when I was about twelve. All of the boys from the neighborhood church and all of their friends and cousins, anybody who wanted to come and could get twenty dollars together, could come and enjoy a week of swimming and baseball and hot dogs and horses and mostly just fun and foolishness. Yeah, we knew that we would be preached to a little bit, but we could endure that. We brought shaving cream so we could squirt each other and old pillows for our pillow fights, and it was going to be such a great time with no parents and no girls, just twelve-year-old boys and a few men that they called "counselors."

Bobby was a little bit different from the rest of us. His clothes were old and tattered, his teeth were very crooked, and he talked funny. Whereas everyone else had a suitcase, he kept his stuff in a brown grocery bag. The "cool" kids picked on him and made fun of him. Those of us who were not so cool were so glad that Bobby was there. "Better him than us" was our attitude. We felt relief that we weren't the ones being singled out for ridicule.

What a miserable life Bobby had that week. I remember how bravely he tried to take what the other kids dished out. It was hard to see him go through that because I knew a little of how it felt. I remembered the sting of being the last one chosen for a game of baseball or football. Believe me, you are thankful when somebody comes along who is worse. Bobby was the one who insulated me and a few others from being the most uncool.

Even now I am reluctant to admit that I, who understood what it meant to feel rejected, did not have the courage to stand up for Bobby. Knowing something of how he felt, why didn't I care what was happening to him? Instead, when tricks were played on him, we laughed extra loud. Whatever the cool kids did to him we did too. I was a part of the "in" group. I belonged!

On one of the last nights of the camp, something happened that none of us would ever forget. Somebody had thought up a secret plot against Bobby. One person was appointed to be friendly to him and engage him in conversation outside while the rest of us absolutely destroyed all of his stuff. Everything he had: all the crafts he had made, his clothes, his sheets and blankets, everything but his Bible, we all tore to shreds. (Oh what hypocrites we were that we wouldn't damage his Bible but thought so little of damaging his spirit!)

When Bobby came in, we all hid and watched. I will always remember watching Bobby as he discovered what had happened. This poor, pathetic boy was so broken that he wailed loudly and just fell on the cabin floor, shaking and sobbing and crying with a broken heart that we had broken.

Things got really quiet as Bobby lay in a fetal position, trembling and devastated.

Suddenly, things weren't very funny any more. Suddenly, nobody was "cool."

Suddenly, we all wished that we had not even come to camp. I felt a very sick feeling in my stomach. I couldn't believe that I had taken part in this incredible cruelty.

When the camp counselors came over, they were furious! Some of them wanted to just take us all home right then. They were trying to think of some way to make us pay for what we had done. We knew that we were in trouble, and we deserved punishment and even welcomed it. A fitting punishment would at least bring some kind of closure to the guilt we felt. Then the head counselor came up with an idea that still today rings in my memory. Things were very quiet as we hung our heads in shame.

Slowly and thoughtfully, he spoke. *"Boys, you may think that you got by with something here, but I assure you that you didn't get by with anything. I'm going to give you the worst punishment that I can possibly give. I'm not going to do anything to you, because nothing can pay back the harm that you have caused. I am sentencing each of you to a lifetime of remembering what you have done. I hope and pray that you will never ever forget this. Now go to bed."*

Nobody had to tell us that this indeed was the worst possible punishment. As we went to bed, there were no pillow fights, no shaving cream battles, no laughter, and very few words. Sometime in the middle of the night one of the counselors took Bobby home, and I never saw him again.

Long, long ago a prophet penned the words about one who would be "despised and rejected by men — a man of sorrows, acquainted with grief." What was done to Him was done by people like me. God knows the remorse that I feel. I truly believe, as much as it is possible for me to believe it, that I have been forgiven.

But, Bobby... Bobby... Where are you?

7

Absurdity in My Family

"I have asked God to please let me do one special thing when I get to see my dad again. I want to introduce these three men to him."

My father was a good man. Of course, not a perfect man, but one who came from a very difficult background and lived a life that was humble, and helped many others along the way. I was always very proud of him. He never told me the importance of getting up and going to work every day, but he showed me by example. Working at the steel mills in Birmingham for forty-two years, the only time I remember that he didn't go to work was when he was in the hospital. Dad took good care of his family, and he loved me a lot. I loved him, and I miss him.

But I want to tell you briefly about three very special men who greatly affected my young life.

I never knew the name of the first one at all. The second man I only knew by his first name, and the third one I only knew by his last name. All three of them touched my life in unusual ways at unusual times, each one five years apart from the other, exactly when I was seven... then when I was twelve... and then when I was seventeen.

I am so thankful that these men came into my life when they did. Yet, incredibly, my father did not want to know them, see them, or hear about them. I know it sounds strange, but he absolutely refused even to listen to the stories that I am about to tell you.

The first one, whose name I never knew, came into my life and back out in less than a minute's time. I was a seven-year-old boy, somewhere in a lake or a huge deep swimming pool. It was the middle of a hot summer. Somehow I got out into water that was over my head, and I couldn't swim. I remember gasping for breath, bouncing my feet on the bottom of the pool or lake, and reaching up with my hand no longer able to reach the surface. I felt as if everyone was a mile away, and the sounds of the people swimming faded away into quietness as I went under into the darkness. Nobody was aware that I was about to drown. Absolute panic began to seize me, and I recall thinking that "Right here, right now, I am just a little boy, and I am going to die!"

Just at that moment when I couldn't find the surface and couldn't even gasp for any more air, this man came through the water with a "whoosh," and immediately took me in his incredibly strong arms, carrying me safely to shore! He then sat me down at the water's edge and quickly disappeared. I remember that I never had the chance to even thank him before he was gone. God bless that young man who literally saved my life! I never knew his name at all.

But I remember that when I got home and told my father, he didn't even want to hear about it.

The second man was just called Ernie. I was twelve years old and had a job in Constantine's restaurant in Birmingham. I remember that I wanted to work there because they served a fantastic lemon ice-box pie! Other boys had the jobs of waiting on customers in their cars, while I was the "inside man," preparing the orders for milk shakes and cheeseburgers so the curb-hops could deliver them to the parking lot. Ernie was the cook.

What was so special about Ernie the cook? Just that he was the first adult to ever talk to me and treat me like I was an adult! He spoke with me, on my own level, not *at* me like I was just a dumb kid. He even actually listened to me! With him I felt valued and appreciated. Ernie worked there for many years with a quiet confidence and maturity that earned him respect from everyone. He had a great outlook on life. You didn't work *for* him, and he didn't work *for* you. He worked *with* you. After I left that job, I even came back a few times, just to see Ernie.

But strangely, when I told my father that Ernie was my friend, he strongly disapproved. Dad never even wanted to meet Ernie.

The third man who had such a great effect on my life was known as "Mister Meredith." I will never forget the day we met. I was seventeen, had just finished high school, and joined the U.S. Coast Guard. I was flown to California, and Mister Meredith met us at the entrance to the Coast Guard base in Alameda. He was six foot three, 230 pounds of muscle and steel. He asked me my name, and I told him, "Lee." He bellowed, "You mean Lee, SIR, don't you?" My father had instructed me *not* to call him "sir," so I said no, I don't mean "sir," just "Lee."

Mister Meredith picked me up and shook me until my

teeth rattled and my heels kicked against my butt. He asked me if I wanted to live to see another day, and I whimpered, "Yes, sir!"

From that time on, through the next three months of boot camp, Mister Meredith taught me strength of character, endurance, and discipline. He was my company commander, and he was the best. I learned so much from him, and he must have forgiven me for that first time we met, because he let me live. And I know that if I saw him today, I would still call him "sir!" The respect I have for him will never go away.

Unfortunately, my father felt differently.

Perhaps you are wondering why my dad, a really good man in so many ways, would not even want to hear about these men. One had saved my life, one had been a great friend, and one had taught me so much. Yet, my father who loved me told me not to honor them, befriend them, or show them respect. Why would he be that way? Would you like to guess?

The answer... an answer that is beyond all absurdity... was simply this: their skin was black.

That was it. For no other reason than their color, Dad rejected these men who had meant so much to me.

Over the years, I have learned to appreciate the good that was in my father while totally repudiating his ridiculous racial prejudice. He died in 1984, and even before his death many of those attitudes changed.

But can I tell you one more secret? I have dreamed about this, and I have asked God to please let me do one special thing when I get to see my dad again.

I want to introduce these three men to him.

I want to say, "Look, Dad, this is the man who saved my

life when I was drowning! And this is my friend Ernie!"

And my father will give them a big hug and say "Thank you!"

Then I will introduce my father to Mister Meredith.

And my dad will look up at him and say, "Pleased to meet you, sir!"

8

American Idols

"Good news for the pizza delivery boy, the mom trying to get the kids ready for school, and the man driving the same old pickup truck to work every day."

A while back, I turned on the television and wound up watching a program that almost made me cry. It was one of the "American Idol" auditions. Since that time, I have become hooked on that show. But this particular program focused on many of the rejects – the worst singers to have entered the try-outs.

I think that it was meant to be comical, and it actually was because these people were just awful singers! But, somehow, these contestants had never been told how terrible they really were. They had the planned stylish moves, some cool costumes, and most of all, big dreams of being the next nationwide celebrity. Nobody had told them, however, the brutal, honest truth that they just could not sing at all. (I don't mean that they were just not good enough to be professional singers. I mean that they were tone-deaf, or as we say down South, they "couldn't carry a tune in a bucket!")

The judges, upon hearing them, held nothing back, and were, in fact, merciless and even sarcastic. "Whoever told you that you could sing lied to you," one said. "I would rather hear a cow give birth than to hear you sing! Have pity on the world and do something else, *anything* else, with your life! You have *no talent* for singing!"

Some of the contestants argued back that they indeed could sing. They were in denial of the most obvious fact.

Some of them said that they were having a bad day, or it just wasn't the right song. They, too, were in denial.

Some tried to take the news bravely, but said that their "dream will not die," and they would work harder to become a good singer. The judges told them frankly that it could never happen, that a certain innate talent was missing, and that they might get better, but they would never be good, much less great.

The judges were right.

However, what almost made me cry was not the dozens of contestants who were in denial, but the ones who, for the first time ever, were told the obvious truth and accepted it. The judges pulled no punches in telling them the shocking truth that no one had told them before... that they were, in fact, horrible singers.

And these contestants suddenly realized that, as painful as it was... it was the bitter truth.

I was embarrassed for them.

There, in front of millions of viewers, their hearts were

broken, their talents were ridiculed, and their dreams were dashed onto the rocks. The unavoidable reality caved in on them, and it was not a pretty sight. One very handsome young man literally fell to the floor, overcome with sorrow. Utterly devastated, he wailed loudly for more than a full minute. It seemed much longer.

Sitting there, just watching it, I wanted to cry. I felt guilty for being entertained by this intrusion into his overwhelming grief.

I could go a lot of directions with this story. I could talk about the fact that TV appeals to the worst of our nature when it gets us to laugh *at*, instead of *with*, other people. That is certainly true.

Or, I could talk about the fact that we all have limitations, areas in which we have no talent, and we need to admit that there are some things we will never be good at. Find out what you can do well, and work at becoming even better. But when you find something that you could never do well, let somebody else handle that.

(This does not mean that you can get by with saying you have "no talent" to cut grass or wash dishes! I tried that excuse, and it doesn't work!)

I could comment on the unintended cruelty of the family and friends of these singers, friends who never had the courage to tell their "loved ones" the truth that they couldn't sing a lick! It would have been kinder to tell them gently before they made fools of themselves.

But instead, I would like to make a different point by asking some important questions:

Are Carrie and Kelly and Taylor and Reuben and the other great singing talents on "American Idol," actually better people than these embarrassed young ladies and gentlemen who couldn't carry a note?

Are J. Lo and Brad, and all the other celebrities in the movies and entertainment and sports, just better human beings than all the rest of us?

If someone is able to sing or dance, or act, or just look so beautiful, are they really different from us in ways that really count?

If a man can quickly carry a bag of air across a line of chalk... or hit a small sphere with a big stick... or slam a round ball through a hoop... or knock a little ball into a cup in the ground... does that make him just worlds above the masses of "average" humanity? Is his life innately more valuable than yours or mine?

While admiring and enjoying their talents, I, for one, am getting weary of the fawning. I don't really care what size pool Paris Hilton has, or how many diamonds Madonna has, or who Ben is engaged to now. I don't need to know who designed the dress or who fixed the hair. And... please trust me... I am not jealous!

But on the other hand, I have some really good news for all of the rest of you.

Good news for you who struggle to pay your bills, who have bad hair days, and who can't seem to lose those pounds.

Good news for all of you who can't slam-dunk a ball, and who will never see Hollywood.

Good news for the pizza delivery boy... the mom trying to get the kids ready for school... and the man driving the same old pickup truck to work every day:

There is only one whose opinion really matters.

There's only one who has the right and power and wisdom to be the judge of everyone.

And to Him you are just as important... just as valuable... just as good... and just as significant as Cher, or Liz, or Brad, or 'Magic,' or Tiger. Or Carrie or Adam or Kelly.

Actually the last time I checked, He didn't really care much for idols.

9

An "A" For Life

*"Some thought there had to be a 'catch.' But there
was no catch. He really meant it."*

A friend of mine, Steve Brown, is a very gifted seminary
professor. He has helped me and thousands of others to better
understand the awesome, radical, and amazing nature of the
grace of God.

When I was a worn out Pharisee, exhausted from years of
trying to carry out a performance-oriented life and to perpetu-
ate a performance-oriented ministry, I attended one of his semi-
nars and ran smack-dab into the truth of what grace is really all
about.

I realized that, though I believed that I was "saved by
grace," I didn't have a clue when it came to living by grace. Instead of being set free, my faulty understanding of religion had
wound me up so tight that I was making everybody, especially
myself, totally miserable. One of the reasons that I make such a

fuss about freedom and grace is that I know what it is like to try, year after year, to live without it.

At the very beginning of the new semester in one of his classes, Steve said something like this to all of the students in that class:

"I have some wonderful news for you today! At the end of this semester, every one of you will receive, for your final grade, an A. Whether you deserve it or not, it doesn't matter. Whether you work hard or get lazy, I am hereby on this day promising and guaranteeing for you nothing less than an A for this course!"

The members of the class couldn't believe their ears at first, but once they became convinced that Steve was on the level, they were thrilled! Some thought there had to be a catch. But there was no catch. He really meant it.

He went on to say:

"How much you get from this course is up to you. If you come to class and pay attention, do the assignments and study hard, you will benefit much from the class. As a result, you will probably enjoy it more, and what you learn here can also be used to benefit others in your life. I sincerely hope that you will do this, and will really put yourself into it. But, regardless, I have promised you a gift — the grade of A. So since the pressure is off, have fun with it."

From what I understand, the administrators called him in and said that he couldn't do that, but he told them that he had already done it!

I'm sure that what my friend was doing was (by example) teaching these students a lesson in grace that they will never forget. That was exactly Steve's point.

I used to think that when God said, "Thou shalt not," that it meant that He would be very very angry with us if we disobeyed His authority because He wanted to show us who was the boss. Now I see that it is because He cares for us and doesn't want us to hurt ourselves.

When you told your children not to play in the street, not to fill up on candy bars, and not to touch that sharp broken glass or jump out the window or anything else like that, it was because you loved your kids and didn't want to see them enter into an unhappy experience. God does us the same way. But if and when they do whatever they want and start to scream and cry, you still love them and they are still yours. Don't you suppose God is the same way with his kids?

We live in a world that includes laws of cause and effect. All of our actions have consequences. God loves us unconditionally, but the laws of the universe will not be suspended for our sake. You may think that you are invincible until "your time" comes, but I promise you that if you make it a habit to drink anti-freeze and stand in the freeway, your time will come a lot sooner.

Putting his thoughts about grace into a dramatic illustration, Steve put it this way:

"God asked, 'What would you do if I told you that I had decided to give you an A for your entire life, even though you don't deserve it?' And I answered, 'Really?' and He said, 'Yes, really!'

"Then I said, 'Well, first, I would be very glad!' And God said, 'Okay, and then what?' and I said that I would then get some rest.

"'And then?'

"Well, then I think that I would just try to tell everybody

*how wonderful and gracious you are to give me something for
my whole life that I could never earn or deserve, and I didn't
even have to work for it!"*

Then Steve said that it seemed that God really liked that
plan a lot, that it was great and simple enough that anybody
could do it. It's a plan I think I can follow, too!

So friends, I have some really wonderful news:

Because of the love of the One who died and rose again,
you have been offered an A for life! You don't have to worry
about your final grade.

Of course, your life will have much more meaning, much
more joy, and be more beneficial and useful if you show up,
study, pay attention, and learn your assignments. But when you
graduate, it will all be by amazing grace!

I hope that you can believe this. If you do, rejoice in it
with all your heart, that you have been graced enough to "get
it."

John Newton once wrote that not only is grace a free gift,
but that being able to see that it is a free gift is a gift in itself.

Once a lady said to me, "The way that you tell it... I'm
sorry, but that's just too good to be true!" As far as I know, she
never changed her mind.

But it is true. You can stop trying and start trusting. You
can "get some rest" and then tell everybody, in a gentle, loving
and patient way, that there's nothing they have to do because
it's already done, nothing they have to pay because it's already
paid.

In all that the books that I have ever read, this (from Paul
Tillich) is one of my favorite quotes:

"We cannot transform our lives, unless we allow them to

be transformed by that stroke of grace. It happens; or it does not happen. And certainly it does not happen if we try to force it upon ourselves, just as it shall not happen so long as we think, in our self-complacency, that we have no need of it. Grace strikes us when we are in great pain and restlessness. It strikes us when we walk through the dark valley of a meaningless and empty life. It strikes us when we feel that our separation is deeper than usual, because we have violated another life, a life which we loved, or from which we were estranged. It strikes us when our disgust for our own being, our indifference, our weakness, our hostility, and our lack of direction and composure have become intolerable to us. It strikes us when, year after year, the longed-for perfection of life does not appear, when the old compulsions reign within us as they have for decades, when despair destroys all joy and courage. Sometimes at that moment a wave of light breaks into our darkness, and it is as though a voice were saying: 'You are accepted. You are accepted, accepted by that which is greater than you, and the name of which you do not know. Do not ask for the name now; perhaps you will find it later. Do not try to do anything now; perhaps later you will do much. Do not seek for anything; do not perform anything; do not intend anything. Simply accept the fact that you are accepted!' If that happens to us, we experience grace. After such an experience we may not be better than before, and we may not believe more than before. But everything is transformed. In that moment, grace conquers sin, and reconciliation bridges the gulf of estrangement. And nothing is demanded of this experience, no religious or moral or intellectual presupposition, nothing but acceptance."

Can you believe it? Congratulations... you've got an A!

10

Another Parable: "A Tale of Two Churches"

"There are even some people there that don't feel like they have been to church unless they are 'raked over the coals.' Leave them alone. Just calmly and quickly make a U-turn, and head for Elm Street."

It was the best of churches, and it was the worst of churches.

Upon observing Pine Street Church and Elm Street Church, the buildings looked about the same, the communities were about the same, the budgets were about the same, and they belonged to the same denomination.

There was one thing, though, that made them different. Pine Street Church had something that Elm Street didn't have. Elm Street didn't have it and didn't want it. Pine Street, however, felt that they just really couldn't function, couldn't grow, and couldn't be faithful or fruitful without it.

I visited Pine Street one Sunday and noticed that they were in a big attendance drive to be followed by an evangelistic crusade. The Reverend Taylor, the pastor of Pine Street, shook my hand vigorously and motioned for an usher to fill out a card with my address and church membership status. I gave them the information that they asked for. Then I was escorted into a classroom, where everyone was reminded that we all needed to read our Bibles daily, give a tithe or offering, and study the lesson so the class could get a "hundred percent" grade.

A lady stood up in the class and informed us that this class was the only Sunday school class in the whole church that had not yet won the attendance banner, and it was getting embarrassing. Then we had a lesson on the faithfulness of God, and the teacher told us that since God was faithful to us, we should certainly be faithful to the church.

We were even told that in order for God to bless our finances, we must bring all the tithes (ten percent of our income) to the "storehouse" which was the church. It was very simple. We could be financially blessed, or we could be financially cursed. It all depended on whether we tithed that ten percent.

Afterward, we were reminded of the evangelistic crusade that was starting, and of how ashamed we should be if we didn't come back every night and bring others with us. Before the class ended, the teacher asked for all who would come back that night to raise their hands. Since everyone else raised a hand, I raised mine, too. Some of the people in the class looked at me and smiled.

Pastor Taylor introduced the evangelist for the week, exhorting us to faithfulness, high attendance, and to give an extra-generous offering for this "greatly-used man of God." When the evangelist stood to preach, he told us some amazing stories. We were told that hell was thousands of degrees hot. He asked us did we want to go there, and if not, did we want our family and friends to go there? He told us of a man who had put off his "decision" for one more day, and then was killed in a car wreck before he had another chance.

He then related to us that the voice of God himself had told him to warn us that the same thing might happen to any of us before the week was over!

At the end, we sang several verses of a song, and some people came to the front to pray. But apparently it wasn't enough people, because Pastor Taylor then said some things that got many more people to come. He told the children that their mothers would be proud if they came forward. Then he told us that if we didn't come to pray we obviously didn't care if people went to hell. Finally, he said that since most of the people were now at the altar, the rest of us should certainly feel ashamed.

Herb down at the barbershop told me last week that Pastor Taylor is in trouble at Pine Street because some of the people think the church isn't growing fast enough. Herb said that this crusade is probably the pastor's last chance to get some results before the board asks him to leave.

Finally, around 12:30 the service was over, and I left Pine Street Church feeling exhausted. It had been a while since I had been to church, and I had forgotten what an ordeal it could be. I felt that I was a big disappointment to God, that I was not very faithful, and that He was probably quite angry with me. Even though I had raised my hand and promised, I did not return that night. I felt even worse about lying to them, but I just couldn't make myself go through another service. I guessed that I was just not very "spiritual." Really, I didn't want to go back to Pine Street any more.

A few Sundays passed before I went to church again, and this time I visited Elm Street Church. Frankly, I was getting ready to endure another round of a similar ordeal.

But things were very different at Elm Street. Nobody made me fill out a card or stand up and wear a ribbon. I can't really describe it, but here at Elm Street things were more relaxed. There was really not anything special about it, except it felt happy and peaceful. The music was good, but no better than at Pine Street.

The pastor, the Reverend Miller, was friendly but not pushy. He was not the entertaining preacher that the evangelist over at Pine Street had been, but there was sincerity there. Someone asked him a question, and he actually answered, "I don't know!" There was a certain freedom, as if nobody expected him to have all the answers. In one of the study sessions one member said something about "embracing mystery," meaning that there are some things about God we cannot understand, and some questions we cannot answer, and that it was okay!

At Elm Street, no individual or group seemed to be more important than the others were. There was a lot of laughter. Some of the people asked me about my job and about my family. Pastor Miller asked if the church could be of help to me in any way. A young man even told me that the church had been "very honored" by my coming to Elm Street!

They didn't try to get me to do anything. Nobody implied that my love for God was equated with my involvement in the church. They were just glad to be there, and glad that I was with them for that day. I felt that I was among people who were honest and open and real. I didn't feel guilty or ashamed or embarrassed or condemned. I knew that I would come back again to Elm Street Church.

At the beginning of this "tale of two churches," I said that there was something that Pine Street had that Elm Street didn't have. I said that Pine Street Church felt that they couldn't grow or function without it, but that Elm Street Church did not want it.

The "it" that I am talking about is called "manipulation" — putting all kinds of pressure on people to get them to do what they don't really want to do.

Pine Street Church manipulated people through fear, shame, intimidation, guilt, pride, competition, and even greed. Elm Street, on the other hand, did not want to manipulate anybody. It was as different as daylight and dark. They both wanted to do good things, but one church chose force, while the other chose freedom.

Churches like Pine Street will never be satisfied and will never be happy. And they won't let anybody else be, either. Sadly, they really seem to think that this is "serving the Lord," that this is the Christian life.

At Elm Street Church I can find what I really need – a God who loves and accepts me purely by grace, and people who are learning to do the same. No pressure to perform, nothing to pretend, nothing to prove, nothing to force on anybody else.

I hope that at some time in your life you will encounter an Elm Street Church.

If you're looking for one and you find yourself on Pine Street, don't panic and run off the road.

Don't get mad at them; they mean well. They think they

are right and they will probably never change.

There are even some people there that don't feel like they have "been to church" unless they are "raked over the coals." So leave them alone.

But *do* leave them. Just calmly and quickly make a U-turn, and head for Elm Street.

[While I am on the subject of manipulation, please permit me to add a few more comments. Use it as a checklist in case you somehow wind up on Pine Street. I have become so "turned off" by manipulation (especially in the name of Christ) that I can smell the stink of it a mile away. Once I told God that any time it happens I would walk out! I'll leave it to you to figure out that God probably walked out before I did. But anyhow, here is the same truth of "A Tale of Two Churches" put in more straightforward form.]

Many times in my life it has been a delightful experience to go to church. The laughter and tears, the truth we build our lives upon, the joyful and uplifting music, the friendships and the opportunity for spiritual growth — all these things and more can make going to church a very rewarding experience. The church I attend is like Elm Street, and it is really a refreshing place!

Nevertheless, this abusive and anti-Christian ploy is regularly practiced inside the walls of so many of our churches. I have had it done to me. And I'm sad to admit that I have done it myself.

But, in spite of our good religious motives, manipulation is a wrongful act of control upon others. It is contrary to grace, incompatible with freedom, disrespectful of human dignity, and diametrically opposed to love.

Sometimes, as at Pine Street Church, a person in leadership is under pressure to "get results," making it a huge temptation to resort to this practice. There are many fine churches where manipulation is avoided, but I have included a few examples of manipulation that, alas, may sound too familiar:

"After all that the Lord has done for you, can't you at least come back for the evening service?"

"Don't you want God to bless your finances? How can He if you don't tithe?"

"Send in all you can, and He will give you all you need!" (Oh, by the way — you're giving to God, but make the check out to us, at our address!)

"Your mother will be so proud of you when you join the church!"

"Aren't you ashamed wearing those old clothes when everybody else is dressed nice?"

"God told me that you're supposed to do this!"

"Our class has not won the attendance contest in over a year, and we should be embarrassed about it. How do you think the Lord feels about this?"

"I talked to a man about his decision. He put it off for one more day, and the next thing I knew he was dead! It could happen to you, so don't wait!"

"All of you who will promise to come back again tomorrow night, stand up!"

"We can't be a hundred percent unless everybody gets here on time and studies the lesson and brings an offering!"

"They say that hell is a thousand times hotter than a furnace. Do you want to go there? Do you want others to go there?"

"Don't you think God is ashamed of this old carpet, these bad lights, and this old building?"

"Everybody else is coming to the altar to pray. Aren't you going to join them? What will they think of you?"

"God has been faithful to you, so won't you be faithful to Him by coming to all the services?"

"What are you going to say when you stand before God and He looks at your checkbook?"

I'm sure that you could add others to this list. When manipulation is practiced, true and joyful motivation disappears, and only strife and fear and guilt and pressure remain. The felt presence of Spirit of the Lord will be conspicuously absent. Loving God becomes equated not with how we treat our fellow man but with how involved we are in the institutional church.

The worst part of all of this crass manipulation in churches is that it hurts and abuses our most vulnerable and trusting people. They even get the idea that God endorses manipulation, when in fact He hates it.

Most of us are starving to be accepted and loved as we are, even with all our flaws and sins and inconsistencies. I believe that whenever we can find that, we will *want* to come to church! And, eventually, we might even get better, under grace.

Meanwhile, beware the manipulators.

11

Be It Ever So Humble

*"The ghosts of the past, the remembrance of special
people and times and places, are never really far from
our thoughts. We can cherish the memories, but we
cannot go back to a place that no longer exists."*

People are always coming up with new lists for just about
anything you can imagine. A few years ago someone compiled
a list of "the worst places to live in the United States." This
particular reporter, acting on limited information, determined
that the very worst city on the list was Steubenville, Ohio.

Now I have never been to Steubenville, but I can understand what happened next. The good people of the town were
outraged! Very quickly and enthusiastically they began to tell
everyone about their great history, the educational opportunities, the beautiful landmarks, the nice restaurants, and the famous people who came from Steubenville. I was surprised to
learn that Steubenville was the hometown of some really fine
talent, such as baseball pitcher Rollie Fingers and entertainer
Dean Martin. Roy Rogers and Clark Gable came from towns

just down the road from there. It is the home of Franciscan University. People in Steubenville, Ohio, think that it is the best place in the world to live. They told the man who wrote the article that if he didn't like it, the same horse he rode in on could also take him back to wherever he wanted to go, and if he was heading east, to not let the door hit him on the west side.

Whoever you are and wherever you live, it is likely that you have a lot of pride in your hometown, your school, your football team, and other things associated with "home." That is not bad — it is good! We are who we are, largely because of where we came from.

We are bound together with the land and the faces and the places where we have lived our lives. My wife remembers that even when times were hard she enjoyed the sights and scents of the orange groves and the mango trees, the grapefruits and the avocadoes of South Florida. She will never get the sand out of her shoes. Anything below sixty degrees is so cold she says she is "freezing!"

On the other hand, I was raised in a working-class family in Birmingham, where my father worked in the steel mills for over forty years.

Some people might say that Birmingham was a bad place to have to live. Well, they are definitely a few fries short of a Happy Meal!

The smell of soot and coal dust and molten metal, believe it or not, is very pleasant to me! As I grew up, we ate well as long as the blast furnaces were putting that beautiful smoke into the air!

We lived on a steep hill overlooking one of the huge furnaces in the distance, and, from our front porch, we could always see the fire as it burned day and night. When I was a very

small boy I once visited my cousins in Atlanta, and my first
question when I got to their front porch was, "Where's your
fire?" I thought everybody was supposed to have an iron-melt-
ing furnace to look at!

Home, whether the big city or the small town or the country community, was the place where we laughed and we cried,
we worked and we played, we loved and we fought, we broke
up and we made up.

Home is where we first heard Hank Williams and Patsy
Cline, Elvis and Buddy Holly, Marty Robbins or Simon and
Garfunkel, Fleetwood Mac or Pink Floyd.

Home is where we buried our sweet old bird dog, where
we walked the aisle in a summer revival, and where we hung
out until midnight at the Dairy Queen.

Home is the place where we fell in love "forever," and it
actually lasted for three months.

Home is a special place, not because of beautiful scenery
and famous celebrities, but because it is the place where we developed relationships with the ones who lived there. It is a
great place, not because of the standard of living or the cultural
opportunities, but because its soil contains our blood and sweat
and tears. It is unique and different and better than all other
places because it is a part of us and we are a part of it. We
poured our lives into just trying to survive there, and the very
struggle of it all helped us to bond to the people and the places,
the dirt and the concrete, the smells and the sights and the
sounds of home.

Recently, I drove back through what was left of the old
Birmingham neighborhood.

Our old house still stands as a shabby shack.

The blast furnaces are abandoned, and the fire went out a
long time ago.

The school I attended is a run-down empty shell.

A freeway now covers the park where we played baseball.

It's sad to see that things have changed when the way they were is so much a part of who we are.

The ghosts of the past, the remembrance of special people and special times and special places, are never really far from our thoughts. We can cherish the memories, but we cannot go back to a place that no longer exists.

Not only have those places changed, but we have changed, too. Let us find joy in living the life that is given to us now.

But somewhere deep inside all of us there is a yearning for a place where we really know that we belong and are known and are missed and are always welcome – a place where there is love and peace, laughter and joy, satisfaction and fulfillment. We dream of a place where the bad people will be good and the good people will be humble! We hear the faint echo of perfect music. We catch a fleeing glimpse of incredible beauty.

We long for more... much more.

I am persuaded that C.S. Lewis was right when he said that the presence of thirst means there is water somewhere, that the same One who placed this deep desire within us for such a beautiful place has also prepared such a place for us, somewhere, some day.

I don't know how far it will be from Steubenville. I think it may be a little closer to Birmingham!

But such a place, wherever it is, is not very far from any of us who long for it.

And when we do see it, we will then know that we are really... finally... home.

12

Call From the Wizard of Oz

*"Once you leave Kansas there are really no
experts to be found."*

In all of the books that followed,

Dorothy always came back to Oz,

for somehow she knew that Kansas

was not really home because

a new world had opened unto her

where dreams and fantasies come true,

and never again would the shallow and mundane

satisfy her – for now she knew –

that despite small men behind curtains

she had heard in her heart a call

quietly beckoning her to the True Wizard,

The Greatest Wizard of all.

Somewhere this side of the rainbow we seem to have lost or misplaced our sense of adventure. We take no risks, upset no apple carts, ask no embarrassing questions, and express no doubts that we have all the answers. We play it safe, stuff our brains with clichés, and don't dare go into unfamiliar territory. Every mystery must be solved. Every movie must have a satisfactory ending. Every song must resolve into a major chord. Every book must have an epilogue that ties up all loose ends. We want it neat and tidy with nothing left out of place.

I have come to believe that the neatly packaged life is no life at all, and neatly packaged faith is no faith at all, and certainly I should know that the neatly packaged god is no god at all.

If you can answer all the questions and explain all the difficulties about God, you had better get you a bigger one because the one you have is not God.

Author Brennan Manning says in "Ruthless Trust" that truth cannot be left in the hands of theologians and purely logical people, but that we must "bring in the artists, the mystics, and the clowns." They are here to remind you and me that life is to be enjoyed, that chances are worth taking, that we will never get it all figured out, and that it is okay that we are not controlling things.

The artists teach us that God is the author of all beauty, and He delights in His creation.

The mystics show us that truth is found not so much in proposition as in experience.

The clowns illustrate to us that God is not an uptight and angry bookkeeper, but is adventurous, passionate, creative, fascinating, and (dare I say it?) fun!

If this is true, it is quite an accomplishment that somehow

we have managed to make church so boring.

I came from a background where I was taught to be "consistent," meaning I was supposed to learn to be predictable and traditional, to always try to "fit in."

No more! Now I am learning, growing, and changing, and I really don't plan to stop! In the process I will sometimes be wrong about things, but it is a risk I am willing to take, because the alternative is to stagnate and die. Sometimes I tell people that if they only want to hear what they already believe, we could have all stayed home. Usually, they listen and consider what is said, and then if it isn't good they can set me straight. I have no desire to be a heretic.

Frederick Buechner writes that "the killjoys, the phonies, the nit-pickers, the holier-than-thous, the loveless and cheerless and irrelevant" are the ones who are quick to claim that they know all of the truth they need to know.

Then he adds this remarkable sentence: "When Jesus is asked who is the greatest in the kingdom of heaven, He reaches into the crowd and pulls out a *child*.... and says unless you can become like that, don't bother to ask!"

I believe that somewhere deep within your soul and mine there is a child like Dorothy who still listens for another voice — a different voice — and faintly feels a longing to go beyond what we can see and understand and explain. We intuitively know that there is more meaning to our lives than to just survive and succeed on the surface.

We are scarecrows desiring a brain... tin men in need of a heart... and lions who desperately want to become brave.

We're looking for the yellow brick road, and we need something or somebody to help us to find it, and, once we have found it, to stay on it.

We know that it's a terrifying endeavor, a very scary trip. When we leave our comfort zone and no longer can settle for "business as usual" in our lives, anything could happen.

There have been times I have glimpsed past the rainbow and turned back because I was afraid to go. But the call would not go away. I hope and pray that it never will.

If you are still breathing, that means that there still are more adventures ahead for you. There are people to meet and to help, there are things to learn, and there are places to go, sights to see, battles to be fought, and tears to be shed.

It's all good, because it means we are still alive and living our lives as they should be lived.

Once you leave Kansas there are really no experts to be found. We are all walking by faith and often stumble and fall.

But if you will read again the lines of my little poem, you'll notice that, after all, it really is not a call to go away.

It is a call to come home.

13

Christian Confession Booth

"We sing 'Amazing Grace,' but we aren't really amazed anymore, and we certainly don't think of ourselves as wretches. I am sorry."

I recently read two books by a great author named Donald Miller. I couldn't put them down and decided immediately to read whatever he might decide to write just as soon as I can get my hands on any of his books.

In his "Blue Like Jazz" he related a story of how his Christian friends, in preparation for a wild "party time" at their college, constructed a makeshift confession booth with a sign that simply said, "sins confessed here." The non-Christian students assumed that after their drunken debauchery, the Christians expected for them to come and confess their sins to the Christians, who would then preach for them to "repent to be forgiven."

Finally, when one of them actually did come into the

booth, he found that things were not at all as he had expected. There in the booth were the Christians, waiting instead to confess *their* sins to this young man!

What an amazing turnaround that was! An almost unheard of scenario that went flying in the face of all assumptions and stereotypes. What a refreshing thing it is when Christians get off their "high horses," get honest, and become vulnerable and open to other people! I believe that we would see some powerful things happen if we did.

But I am not holding my breath, because change doesn't usually come so quickly.

However, to at least make an attempt, let me confess to all of you who do not consider yourselves to be Christians, some of our many sins and offenses, and offer an apology to you for having to endure our shortcomings.

We have become such very poor representatives of this wonderful man we say we are following. He cared about the poor, lived a simple life, always had compassion, and common sinners were loved and accepted by him. We live complicated, materialistic, uncaring lives which often reek of self-righteousness instead of grace. We sing "Amazing Grace," but we aren't really amazed anymore, and we certainly don't think of ourselves as wretches. I am sorry.

Our "Christian" television and radio programs often consist of bizarre manipulation, emotionalism, cheap commercialization, and celebrity worship. Some of our programs make a circus out of the healing of a stopped-up ear, but we don't show you the people who come in and go out in wheelchairs. Some of us preach a God who is more into prosperity on earth than treasures in heaven, more into healing the body than the soul, more into the image of success than the vulnerability of truthfulness. I am sorry. If my idea of a Christian were based on what I see on Christian TV, I will be quick to admit to you that I would never want to become one.

I see us following after some novel and fanciful interpretation, finding secret codes in the Bible, enamored over what will happen to those "left behind," excited over people being slain on the floor, and anything and everything else but the message of God's love and grace and forgiveness. I am sorry.

Our Lord whom we profess to follow shunned the opportunity for political power, for very good reasons that we seem to have forgotten. He refused to become the kind of king that would nail his enemies to the wall. Scripture says that he would not break a bruised reed or snuff out a smoldering wick on a candle. He was always gentle in dealing with broken, wounded people. But many of us are totally obsessed with "defending our rights" as Christians, and become angry or even paranoid if we can't require everyone to embrace our values or pray our prayers. I am sorry.

Watch what kind of angry people show up to defend the display of the Ten Commandments, or prayer in the schools. It can get a little scary, and I am embarrassed, and I am sorry.

We divide into denominations and split churches over some minor differences in method or interpretation, and thereby send confusing, complicated signals to you rather than sharing the love of Christ with you. I am sorry.

I must also apologize for each of us because though we ourselves are sinners, we haven't admitted it enough. We come to church and appear to have it all together in our lives when we don't. We allow people to keep the illusion that we are all good people when we aren't. We are not more worthy than you or better than you are. We are plain people with faults and sins and problems just like you have.

We get divorces. We lose our temper. We view pornography. We cheat on our taxes. We are often afraid, confused, and lonely. We need a lot of grace, a lot of forgiveness, and a lot of help, just like you. I am sorry.

I could go on much longer about the many, many ways we have failed you. I am sorry. We are sorry.

In our Christian Scriptures the apostle Paul says, "Christ Jesus came into the world to save sinners, of whom I am chief." He didn't say, "I was a sinner;" he said, "I am a sinner — the biggest sinner of all!"

Then he told about a savior who loves sinners more than you could ever dream.

If we would look at how all kinds of sinners were welcomed and forgiven by him and how many self-righteous people could not stand to stay around him, we might realize that, if indeed there are "sides" at all, that we are on the wrong side.

But He never said we would not fail Him. He never said that we would not fail you. He did say that He would not fail us. And you can count on Him, even if you can't count on me.

The message is not really about me at all. It's about Him. And if anybody ever needed to hear that message, it is I. I must personally apologize because I, too, have often been the smug, hypocritical one I have been writing about. I am compelled to apologize.

So if we ever meet in a confession booth... please... let me go first.

14

Christmas Is Not Receiving, But Giving

"We were at the mercy of whoever might be coming down the highway on this extremely cold night in this remote area. We had no other choice but to hold on to each other and wait."

It was Christmas morning many years ago. I was a little boy, and times were good in Birmingham. The steel mills were going strong, so "Santa" had been able to afford to bring to my brother Jeff and to me quite a few nice toys, including a brand new tricycle! After we had opened our gifts, the living room was full of new toys and boxes and clothes and wrapping paper. I was elated over all the great stuff that we got. It was a joyful time for the family. I guess that I was about six.

When you're an immature kid as I was, you think everything is good for everybody when things are going well for you. It is pretty much out of character to stop and think about someone else while you are having so much fun. But for some reason, I did the out of character thing. Suddenly, (and I remember this well) I turned to see my father and mother smiling and enjoying this time with us, and it occurred to me that Santa Claus had not brought them anything. I wondered to my dad, "How can you be so happy when you didn't get any presents?" And he said something that just blew me away. "I'm just happy to see *you* get the things you wanted. I didn't want anything, I just wanted for you and Jeff to have what y'all got. That's what makes me happy!"

I remember thinking that it was the craziest thing I had ever heard anybody say. We didn't use these words back then, but now I can say "It just didn't compute." How could he possibly be happy when my brother and I got all the presents, and he got nothing? How totally weird that seemed to me! It's so remarkable how these strange people called parents will invest so much time and money on their children, and sometimes their only reward is a quick laugh or a smile or a thank you, and that, to the parents, is reward enough and makes it worth it all to them.

One of the few Bible verses my daddy knew, and I'm not sure that he even knew it was in the Bible, was this one that he often quoted to me: "It is more blessed to give than to receive." To him, it was not just a verse; it was a way to live.

Fast forward more than thirty years to the bitterly cold Christmas Eve of 1983. My wife and I, along with our little girl and our little boy, were living in Atlanta and were headed to Birmingham to get together with family. My dad had just died just two weeks before. My mother and all my younger brothers and their families were all waiting for us in Alabama.

It had already turned dark when we started out on the trip

from Atlanta, and the temperature had dropped to an extremely cold temperature for the South. It was five degrees. I was driving one of the worst automobiles to ever come out of Detroit - a 1978 Oldsmobile *diesel* sedan! As we traveled that night, the infamous motor on this infamous car started freezing up even as we drove down the highway.

Heading west toward Alabama on Interstate 20, we only made it fifty miles or so when, several miles from the nearest freeway exit, there in the cold dark night, the diesel engine suddenly blew up. One loud "boom," a huge cloud of smoke, and I knew it would never run again.

Standing there in the dark, I stuck my thumb out as the cars and trucks flew by. I looked over at my family. They were shivering in the cold, crying and trying not to panic. Suddenly I realized that they would not last long out here in five-degree weather. I prayed.

"Dear God, I am so afraid and I don't know what to do!" I turned on the headlights of my destroyed car, and called for my wife and children to stand with me beside the highway, with the lights shining on all of us so that the people whizzing by could see that we were a family.

I knew that the battery would soon die in the Oldsmobile, but until it did, we had a little time for all of us to be seen huddling together, hoping to wave somebody down. I hoped that it would be a kind person, knowing that we were at the mercy of whoever might be coming down the highway on this extremely cold night in this remote area. Of course we had no other choice but to hold on to each other and wait.

We didn't have to wait very long. Almost immediately, two cars pulled over. I soon realized that the two drivers were husband and wife, and they had their children with them and were headed home with one car following the other! Some of us got in his car and the rest of us got in hers. The heater on the car felt so good and warm! Equally warming was the song on the radio, "Christmas in Dixie," by the country group "Alabama."

As the song finished, this family began to express to us an ecstatic joy for the great privilege that God had given them to be able to find somebody they could help on the night before Christmas! These people whom we had never met before were so thrilled just to have the opportunity to do something special for someone!

They took us to their home nearby, and gave us food and started a fire in the fireplace. They had a church Christmas party to go to, but they left us in their nice house, and my family watched "It's a Wonderful Life" on their television. Believe it or not, I had never seen it before that night.

When the family got back from their party, they let us spend the night in their house. While my wife and children were sleeping they arranged to take me back to Atlanta and get my work van, and for the towing of my car that had been left by the side of the road. They would not accept any money for anything they did.

Early the next morning, on Christmas day, we headed on in to join my family in Birmingham. Of course, we tried to express our gratitude and thanks to this wonderful family who had no doubt actually saved not only our Christmas but our lives! But they kept saying, "No, no! We want to thank *you* for letting us help you! Thank you for being there — *you* have made this the best Christmas we ever had!"

Of course their attitude just "blew me away!"

As I said, that was 1983, and so many more years have

passed since then. Our children have families, and of course we have terrific grandchildren.

For me, whatever stuff I might get for Christmas doesn't mean much anymore. But I am grateful for the health that I have, and the fact that our marriage has survived these years, and for so many things. If I didn't get any presents at all I don't think it would bother me. Of course I want my children and grandchildren to be well and happy, and for them to have all that they need and some of what they want. That matters so much more than anything you could put under the tree for me.

From the time when I was first riding that new tricycle in Birmingham, so many Christmas celebrations have come and gone. Some of them have been wonderful, and some have been not so good.

I still don't understand all the amazing things that happened on that very first Christmas, when a special baby was born that many of us believe was the Son of God. The incarnation, when "the Word became flesh," is something that is so beautiful and fascinating, and it is beyond my comprehension.

But I am beginning to understand what my daddy meant on that Christmas when I was just a little boy, and what that wonderful couple in West Georgia meant back in 1983. It isn't so hard to compute any more. I think I get it now. It really is more blessed to give than to receive.

Merry Christmas, everyone!

15

Dead Frogs

"We only learned about biology. We learned almost nothing about frogs."

Back in high school, when I was a student in biology class, there was a day when we all were brought in to the laboratory to dissect bull frogs. We were each assigned a partner to work with, and to each pair of students there was given a big dead bullfrog that had obviously been pickled in formaldehyde for a while. The teacher gave us scalpels and other tools, basins of water and a notebook of instructions. For the next two hours we were to cut the carcass of the frog into pieces and make notes of our observations.

We were just like the famous laboratory scientists, but without the white coats.

We peeled back the thick skin of the frog and noticed how it was put together. We took notes on its long legs and webbed feet. We looked at the amazing amphibian lungs and its chest cavity. We dissected the entrails and the heart. When it was done, we felt that we had learned a lot.

But what we learned that day was only biology. The point that I want to make is that we *only* learned about biology.

We learned almost nothing about frogs!

If one wants to learn about frogs, he needs to spend some time among the lily pads, watching the actions, listening to the sounds, learning the habits of these amazing animals.

Observe the eggs, and the stages of tadpole-dom.

See how the adult sneaks up on the insects.

Differentiate between the "burdeeps" and the "ribbits," and discover that there are mating sounds, and warning sounds, and bragging sounds, and happy and sad sounds, and much more!

Watch how their eyes turn and the pupils change.

Notice the colors that they display.

Try to understand the conflicts they encounter.

In short, spend a lot of time with *living* frogs, and you will learn much more than you can get from the scalpel and the notebook in the biology lab.

The reason I am saying all of this is I think there is too much of the "biology lab" approach when it comes to knowing God. For too many years, we have analyzed Scripture as if it were a math book instead of a love letter. Too many of us have sincerely labored under the assumption that if we studied more biblical facts, systematized our theology, drew charts about the end-times, and could answer all the academic questions, that we would know God better and be better and more spiritual people.

I am here to tell you that it doesn't work! I have known some people who have degrees in the subject of God, but did not have much knowledge of the real ways of a living God. At times I have been one of those people.

I also have known people who had very little religious knowledge, but they humbly walked in a loving and powerful relationship with one who had become their closest friend.

I am blessed to have had many years of studying and teaching the Bible. I was at one time a professor of New Testament studies in a Christian college. I don't want to discount the value of knowing the book in any way.

But we are living in a time when most people couldn't care less about our theological analysis or our detailed exposition of Scripture unless there is some living evidence to indicate that He is personally real to us.

To many people, even the stories of Daniel in the lion's den, Noah and the ark, or David and Goliath are looked at as something which, if they happened at all, happened to somebody they don't know, at a time long time ago, in a place far away. Meanwhile, they are struggling with emptiness and meaninglessness in their own lives. They are also worried about paying their bills, keeping their jobs, holding their marriage together, getting drugs away from their kids, and fighting cancer.

They have every gadget and every avenue of communication from cable TV to Internet social networking, but even with all of these distractions, most people know that something is still missing.

The answer they are longing for is not found in knowing the Bible. It is found in knowing the God of the Bible.

So when, by experience, I can give evidence that I really

am acquainted with a living God, one who is great and powerful and awesomely active in my life, I am now finally getting
somewhere! When I am able to tell about a God who can and
does make a difference in my own situation, then I am on the
right track! And when at last I can share that I am learning to
understand his ways and trying to hear his voice... well, now,
that will be exciting! That will get the attention of people!

Of course it is nice to know how God worked in the lives
of people a long time ago. But it is more relevant, up-to-date
and powerful if we can show how He is working in our lives
today.

The world has been trying for some time to tell us that
they have "had it" with church and religion and empty meaningless God-talk. Please don't be angry. Don't write them off.
Don't condemn them to a hot place.

Please just take it as a wake-up call.

They are just trying to tell us what we should have already
known, which is this:

It's time for us to leave the biology lab, and to head for the
frog ponds and the lily pads.

These frog ponds and lily pads can be anywhere. Even in
our own hearts.

16

Down and Out at Second Base

"I was standing just a few feet away as I saw Greg suddenly stand up from the dust and, quickly, with his fist, hit the second baseman in the face!"

"Greg" was the kind of man that absolutely everybody liked. He was just your all-around good guy, a man with genuine Southern charm, who worked hard at his job, loved his family, and served faithfully in his church. Greg was a sportsman who loved to hunt and fish and camp. He was good at football and baseball, both as a player and as a fan. He was competitive to the core. As all sportsmen, he loved to win and hated to lose. He put his whole heart into whatever he did.

When I came to be the minister of the little church he attended, he was very active in the church, and we became friends. He willingly served, and led the congregation in singing the songs from the hymn book.

Every summer our church had a softball team that played

in the local church league, and of course Greg was one of our most enthusiastic and talented players.

Then one Friday afternoon there was a particular game which we played against another church from across town. It started out like any other church league game, and things were going smoothly, with everybody having a good time. There was a smattering of other church members from both sides... wives and kids and neighbors and friends, watching the game. The score was close and both teams were trying hard to win this one.

Greg came to bat and lined a single to right field. He was standing on first base when the next batter hit a slow ground ball to the shortstop. Greg was running from first toward second, and he could see that the throw was going to second to try to force him out. Then, just as the big league players do, he slid hard into second base trying to break up the play.

Actually, as baseball fans know, the runner will not really try to slide into second base at all, but will slide into the player! That is what Greg tried to do.

The second baseman for the other team must have resented this, because he tagged Greg very hard. I was standing just a few feet away as I saw Greg suddenly stand up from the dust and quickly, with his fist, hit the second-baseman in the face ! This other player fought back, landing a solid punch to Greg's eye.

By this time everybody, including the wives in the stands, ran to the field and began pulling the two men away from each other. We ended the game right there. After a few minutes both Greg and the second-baseman caught their breath and cooled off and shook hands. Then they went home covered in dust and dirt and blood, listening as their wives told them what idiots they were.

The next day Greg had a huge black eye... actually a dark bruise that covered half of his face. And Greg had to live with this bruise, answer all the questions as to how it happened, and hear all of the not-so-funny comments from people.

The next day Greg called me and met with me and said, "Pastor, I am so ashamed. I just lost my temper and everybody knows it. I'm supposed to be a Christian example, and I have blown it. I have ruined my testimony for the Lord. I am so sorry. I am resigning from all positions of leadership at the church."

I said to Greg, "You don't need to resign from anything. Yes, you lost your temper and did something that was wrong, but Greg, you are only human! These people in our church are gracious and kind and forgiving. They love you! You have just reminded us that we all are sinners and sometimes we mess things up, and we need forgiveness. Your sin was not any worse than ours... it is just a little harder to hide, since it was in public and you have a black eye that's hard to miss! So why don't you just come on Sunday, and stand up and lead the singing, and whenever you want to you can tell the church what happened, and you can apologize if you wish to. Trust me, they will understand."

The next Sunday morning in church, Greg showed up with this big black eye, and began leading the music. After the first song he explained what had happened and told everybody how sorry he was about it. I will never forget what happened next.

An elderly gentleman stood up and made a little speech about how much Greg had meant to his life, and how it was only right that we should forgive him and accept him and en-courage him. With great enthusiasm, everybody said "amen," and most of the people started to cry. They left their pews and, one by one, walked up to Greg and hugged him! It was really beautiful.

There was no preaching that morning. It wasn't necessary. The people of the church, with their sympathy and their love, preached a better sermon than I could have ever done. I heard later that a very similar thing had happened at the church across town, when their second-baseman stood up!

Repentance. Authenticity. Compassion. Forgiveness. Grace. Isn't that what church is supposed to be about?

And, as always, it is followed by tears and laughter. It is the joy of knowing that, despite our offenses and our unworthiness, we are loved and accepted completely, with no strings attached.

When offenses are forgiven, sometimes people say, "It is as if it never happened."

No... it is better than that! Even our black eyes proclaim the grace and glory of God.

By the way, since I was standing close by and saw the whole thing, I can tell you this for certain:

On Friday, Greg was out at second base. But on Sunday, he was safe at home.

17

Downward Mobility

"I became so angry that I imagined some very creative ways that somebody should punish this incredibly spoiled brat. I personally wanted to drop-kick her across the parking lot!"

Last night on the computer I watched a two-minute video of a teenage girl who, for her birthday, was given a $70,000 Lexus. It was a beautiful, retractable-top convertible. Her mother had it presented to her with a huge ribbon on top and had arranged to give it to her before her party so she could drive it to the party to show to her teenage friends.

Well, I was shocked with disbelief over what happened next! This girl started cursing and crying and complaining! The video had to bleep out her words as she verbally attacked her mother for "ruining her party" by giving it to her ahead of time!

When I went to bed I just couldn't forget her outrageous

ungratefulness! I became so angry that I imagined some very creative ways that somebody should punish this incredibly spoiled little brat. (I personally wanted to drop-kick her across the parking lot!)

I considered that the parents should be held responsible for doing such a poor job of instilling values and character in their child. I thought of how many poor children's lives could have been saved with the money spent on this beautiful extravagant gift that was offered to an undeserving yet ungrateful twit. The unfairness of it all literally kept me awake for a while.

Coincidentally, I had just been reading Richard Foster's fine little book "Freedom of Simplicity," so it didn't take me long to shift to a more introspective view.

I really would like to have spent more time despising this girl, but I had to begin to look into my own heart. Could it be that the reason I was so upset at this was because I am, to some degree, like her? Do I ever demand and expect more than I deserve? Have I been ungrateful for what I have? Have I ever whined and complained when things didn't come together at the exact time I wanted them to?

The answer, regretfully, is yes.

We may not sneer at a gift-Lexus, but most of us are card-carrying (get it?) members of a consumer society that is out of control. ("What's in *your* wallet?")

How many of us see something advertised that we never even knew existed, and suddenly we have "got to have it?"

How many of us have put something in a yard sale, traded something in, or thrown something away simply because it is no longer in style or as nice as the "new and improved" model?

Unfortunately, we have been brainwashed into thinking that we will just be much happier with newer and better stuff. Brainwashed is a strong word, but it is exactly what I mean to say. Advertisers have purposefully manipulated our desires. They have scientifically analyzed us and programmed us to respond just the way they want us to.

We are laboratory rats running through the mazes, jumping through the hoops, and being injected with the poisons. We have all been trained to run as fast as we can on that little drum that does nothing but spin and goes nowhere but in circles. No wonder it's called a "rat race!"

Most of you would probably be as shocked as I was at the video of the spoiled-rotten teenager. It is hard to feel sympathy for such a person, but her actions and attitude betray a very strong discontent... a very deep unhappiness.

Philip Yancey in "Reaching for the Invisible God" refers to a surprising study that examined the level of happiness among the people of the world. The study proved conclusively that the moderately poor are much happier than the richest people! Those who are in dire poverty are the least happy. The wealthy are happier than the poverty-stricken. But, generally, the happiest people of all are those that most of us would call "poor people," those who have only few possessions and only a meager income, So they must depend on each other in the community to survive.

I decided recently to take a voluntary step of downward mobility, agreeing to swap cars with a family member until her baby comes. Yes, my car was fairly nice — not new, but still comfortable. What I got in exchange (for a while) was a 1993 Saturn with over 200,000 miles.

It is a stick-shift with no power steering and crank-up windows. It is scratched and cramped and uncomfortable and slow and out of style.

The good news is that girls see me in that car and wave at me and blow the horn! The bad news is that they are motioning for me to "Get out of the way!"

Also, my friends aren't impressed. And, you know what? I think that I will survive!

Learning to get along with older and cheaper things can be of great benefit if it teaches us to appreciate what we have and to demand less.

I really believe that God wants to work in our lives to change some of our priorities, and to give us the power to be happy with what we have. Paul said that if we have food and clothing, we should be able to be content.

Can we please just stop being lab rats and try to become more thankful for our blessings?

Can we remind ourselves that a grateful heart is a happy heart?

Can we discipline ourselves, at least occasionally, to move *down* the ladder a little bit, instead of up?

One thing I realized last night after I saw the video of that spoiled girl: unless she changes she will always be miserable. People will get fed up with her and drop her like a hot muffler.

Nobody will want to ride in her Lexus unless she gets out first! So I want to become as much unlike her as I possibly can.

I'll try to think about that when I see somebody who has a lot of really nice stuff. I will tell myself that I am on a journey to the happier side of life!

I'm just hoping that this old Saturn can make the trip.

18

Easter At Sunrise

" It doesn't always have to be new, it doesn't always have to be entertaining, and it doesn't have to be the latest modern idea that's going around. "

Just a few days before Easter my wife expressed to me that she would like for us to go to an Easter "sunrise service" to be held outside, down at the edge of Mobile Bay, at a time scheduled for a half hour before dawn.

I said, "Okay, sure!" not really believing that she would follow through with it. I am the "morning person" in our family. She, on the other hand, has a little sign that asks, "Is there life before coffee?"

But, much to my surprise, she woke me up at five o'clock, having made coffee and reminding me that we needed to get ready so we could be there early. About an hour later we arrived with our lawn chairs, joining about two hundred other sleepy-eyed people as we sat beside the bay in the cold and the dark.

There were prayers in the dark, songs in the dark, and beautiful music by a small choir from one of the local churches. Some people were dressed in nice dresses or suits, and some of us were much more casual. As the people gathered, I sat in my lawn chair and wondered what would possess so many of us to gather here at 6 a.m., and what did we expect to see?

The service was very traditional, and it didn't take long before I realized that I would probably not hear or see anything that I had not seen hundreds of times before. Then (please pardon this terrible pun!) it dawned on me!

Really, just at the first glimpse of dawn, I began to understand this: it doesn't always have to be new, it doesn't always have to be entertaining, and it doesn't have to be the latest modern idea that's going around.

In fact, there is something really special about the stability and the routine of the good news of the "old-old story." We had gathered together in the cold of the early morning simply to honor our firmly held belief in resurrection, in life beyond the grave, our belief that there was a man who was more than just a man, who really died, and was really buried, and who really got up and walked again!

As the light began to spread over the dark bay, the words of the minister seemed to take on a vitality and an importance that elicited a quiet but deep joyfulness from within me. The message was beautiful to me, because it had now fallen upon a receptive soul who rejoiced in its simple but powerful truth.

A wonderful thing happened next:

Just as the glow from the sun was beginning to change the appearance of all of our surroundings, as if beckoned by a divine presence, a mixture of birds — gulls and sandpipers and geese and ducks and pelicans — all began to fly toward the sunlight, singing and honking and quacking and chirping and calling with whatever sounds they were created to make!

The minister continued his sermon without mentioning it.

But to me, it seemed that all nature had joined in to share in the presentation of a message of hope restored... that not only on Easter, but *every* sunrise shouts to us a happy message that morning has come, that darkness has vanished and the light is now here, that the mistakes and hurts of yesterday are behind us, that the opportunity to live a new day has been given to us all!

The sea birds, as well as the sparrows and robins and cardinals and finches, all sing the song of a fresh beginning, of a renewed hope, of a bright future! This universal message is echoed throughout nature at sunrise every day! And those of us who took the time to be there were privileged to join in the celebration.

Soon, the service was over, and I carried our lawn chairs back to the car. People loaded up and left. We went back to our busy lives to face the pressures and labors of what sometimes has been called a "rat race."

But the birds stayed behind, singing and honking, quacking and chirping, long after we all had driven away.

I rose early the following Tuesday and drove at dawn back down to that same spot beside the bay. No people were gathered, and, of course, no service was held that day.

But the birds once again showed up and had their own service without us.

I don't think we give enough credit to the birds. Maybe being "bird-brained" is not as dumb as we once thought. They seem to greet the new day with exuberant joyfulness, and they will do it again tomorrow morning and every morning to come until at last their feathered wings can no longer fly and their tiny throats can no longer emit a sound.

Once He said, "Behold the fowls of the air." Early last Easter morning I think I saw a little more of what He was talking about.

No, I don't plan to set my alarm for five o'clock every morning to watch the sunrise at the bay. But I will not wait until next Easter before I go again.

Sunrise services are going on every day!

19

Elusive Humility

"A strange man with nail prints walked into our meeting that day."

Did you hear about the man who was awarded a nice pin for being the most humble person in his church? The next Sunday they took it away from him for one simple reason: because he wore it!

We don't see many books on humility, because those who are qualified to write them don't think that they are qualified, and the rest — well, thinking that they are qualified disqualifies them!

Yet the Scriptures do say that God resists the proud and arrogant, but gives His grace to the humble and broken. That being true, getting humility must be extremely important!

Seriously, I believe that humility is just seeing things as they really are: that we are guilty sinners with no worthiness but that we are the recipients of an unreasonable grace.

God seems to abhor lists and to love stories. The most profound truths cannot be easily broken down to a simple lecture or outline format. We are not usually given a list of rules teaching us how to develop a certain spiritual quality. Instead, we have been given examples and stories and experiences which help us to see the picture.

In the incarnation, God gave us someone who told stories, one who himself lived "the greatest story ever told."

Turning to the Bible, we find that it is a book which is also full of stories.

Although our own lives are full of failures and inconsistencies, He is giving each of us our own different story of a relationship with him.

So, on the subject of humility, I certainly can't break it down into teaching points. I can't teach about it at all without ruining it or losing it. I have almost nothing to say that will help. I can only tell stories.

And of course they can't be stories of my own humility, supposing I had any. For if they were good ones, then I would be proud of them. I would be like the man in the joke, who wrote "Humility and How I Attained It," with many large pictures of himself, "suitable for framing!"

As soon as I wear the pin, somebody will have to take it away!

So elusive is this quality of humility! Many years ago the famous preacher H. A. Ironside, pastor of Moody Church in Chicago, was struggling with pride. Huge crowds came to hear him preach, and it "went to his head." He sensed how wrong that was, so he tried so hard to become more humble.

One day he rigged a big sandwich-board sign which said, "I am a fool for Christ." He wore it all day and walked all over

Chicago as people pointed, whispered, and laughed. All day long he thought to himself, "Finally, I am going to learn to be humble!"

Exhausted at the end of the day, Dr. Ironside removed the sign from his shoulders. Immediately the thought came to him, "Not many people in the whole city of Chicago could have done that!" Once again he felt himself swell with pride, and he knew that his day, and all his efforts, had been wasted.

A few years ago I was in a pastors' fellowship meeting on a Monday morning. Everyone was talking about a big scandal that had just occurred in one of the local churches.

Some members of this church had done something really dumb. As a gag, they had hired a stripper to perform at a birthday party! It turned out to be quite embarrassing for everybody.

They all hoped that the pastor would not find out about it, but of course, he did... on Sunday morning. When the pastor finally did hear about it, he hit the ceiling! He gave these people a scathing rebuke, then resigned from the church on the spot, and walked out without even conducting the morning service!

As you can understand, this ministerial meeting was abuzz with gossip. Many opinions were expressed about whether we should "take our stand" against the church and the "guilty parties," commend the pastor for "taking his stand," or just what should we do.

(By the way, be careful around people who are always "taking their stand.")

There was a lot of talk. Nothing makes us more vocal than a situation when we can talk about somebody who did something that we would "never" do.

When the talk finally subsided, our host called on our director to lead in a prayer.

We were all feeling quite superior and self-righteous that morning — until he prayed. I shall never forget his prayer.

"Lord, please have mercy upon my sinful, sorry self," he began. "Dear God, you know that I fail you so much, so often, so deeply, so carelessly, Lord! I am so sorry for the way I am! I know that it's only because of your love and grace that a sinner like me could ever be forgiven and be your child. I am so ashamed of myself! Oh, please have mercy on me!"

Now, in case you may have missed it, I want to remind you that this man who was praying was in no way associated with the scandal we had been discussing. He was simply looking into his own heart and had found no room to criticize anybody else, and found no reason to feel superior.

Tears began to break out at that pastors' meeting, as each of us began to pray similar prayers. And a strange man with nail prints walked into our meeting that day.

It happened all because one man with stark, radical, genuine humility had dared to expose his heart in public prayer.

The gossip was over. We were finally "minding our own business," which is the business of honesty and repentance concerning our own sin and unworthiness.

Humility: should it really be that hard to come by? If I will be just be honest, don't I have plenty to be humble about? Can't I just look within and begin to see how outrageous it is for me to become proud?

I have been told that the Greek Orthodox Church has a prescribed prayer to pray whenever another brother has sinned. It is the prayer of the publican in the temple: "God, be merciful unto *me*, a sinner."

Amen. And me too.

20

Everything Is Upside Down

"What if we exist for Him, rather than Him existing for us?"

A nice middle-aged man came up to me, and, with tears in his eyes, he related that his life had been changed by something I had said many years ago. I asked what I had said, and when he told me the details, I honestly couldn't remember saying such a thing. But to him it had been powerful, said in the right way and at the right time, and I was grateful that it had happened.

A man and his wife said to me that a few words I had said on the radio had been used to comfort them at a time of sorrow in their lives. I rejoiced.

A lady stopped me in the aisle of a store, and, in tears, said that something I had done was her motivation to keep going and to not give up. It really made me feel good.

A young man called me crying and said that he was promising me that his life was about to change as a result of a column I had written. I was filled with gratitude and encouragement.

But wait – all of these things are true, but they are not by any means the whole truth. I really would rather not tell the whole story, but I must.

The complete truth is that there are also some who, because of me, have been offended. The hypocrisies and inconsistencies of my life have alienated some people. My own selfishness, my controlling ways, my insistence that I was a hundred percent right, have made some people along the way decide that they could not really listen to anything I had to say. That is the part that I don't rejoice in.

There have been times when I wondered if the only real ministry I could ever have would be to serve as a bad example.

It is so hard to consistently help people without turning right around and hurting somebody! I have tried to be sensitive to this, but there is something within our personalities that has a tendency to do harm along with trying to do good.

Am I a great and effective leader and spokesman for truth and for God? Am I a gift to people, a blessing from above, a profound and thoughtful man of truth and faith and love and spirituality?

Or am I a hypocrite, a shyster, a phony, unworthy and unqualified and unable to really help anybody?

The truth is that I am human... which means that I am neither of these, but at times I can seem to be both of these.

And here is the ironic, paradoxical thing, which I hope that I can explain without confusing anybody:

When I think that I'm the good guy — that's when I'm the

bad guy. When I think that I'm the bad guy — then it is more likely I could be the good guy.

If I start to think of myself as good and obedient and right and righteous or if I start to think of myself as "God's gift to poor dumb sinners," I am not the solution to anything. I am the problem. My arrogance will know no bounds. The people I hurt will be many.

And I will think that all of them are wrong, but that I am right.

Of course I don't want to be like that. But it comes pretty quickly on the heels of pride.

On the other hand, if I can remember that I am just a messed up person... often weak, often wrong, often sinful, and always unworthy, and if I can honestly and humbly remember that, then I can help somebody along the way. And I won't even know that I'm doing it until I hear about it later.

Not knowing about it is an important part. There was a time when, if anybody was saying nice things about me, my ears would tune in to that frequency and listen so I could hear every word! Now... Well, now, I am aware that it might be better for everybody if I don't hear too much of that stuff — lest I forget about the rest of the story.

Steve Brown has often said, "The best thing you've got going for you spiritually is your sin... when you know about it. And the worst thing going against you spiritually is your obedience... when you know about it."

Saint Paul put it this way: "I glory in my weaknesses and failures and reproaches, so that the power of Christ may rest upon me, for when I am weak, only then am I strong."

The old spiritual song said it so well: "Not my brother, not my sister, but it's me, oh Lord — standin' in the need of prayer."

And Walt Kelly's Pogo said, "We have come face-to-face with the enemy, and he is us!'

It should be no secret that nobody, but nobody, has a handle on the Almighty.

A famous evangelist used to have himself introduced as "God's man of faith and power" until he died drunk. I have been to "healing" circuses and seen the people leaving, still in their wheelchairs. So if you know everything you need to know about the god you have, and think that you can control him, he is much too small to be the real thing.

Some things will always be a mystery. Some things we will never get right. And as long as we live on this earth, there will be areas in which you and I will really fall on our face.

Accept it. We're not home yet.

And until we really are home, we remain as fallen people in a fallen world, and most of the things about us and about our relationship with God are upside down from what we have always thought.

Whenever I go through the Christian section of a book store, there are always many books on how to let God fix the difficulties of our lives. God is used as a fixer of all of our problems, a remover of the obstacles, an automatic cure for whatever bothers us, and a very good servant who runs our errands.

Here's a radical thought:

What if He were the sovereign Lord over all?

What if He actually wanted us to live for His glory?

What if He knew that I could magnify His grace more beautifully if I sometimes failed in my great plans, and couldn't always handle my problems?

What if He wanted to see me depend on Him day by day, so I was kept just below the poverty line?

What if it really is all about Him instead of all about me?

Do I get myself in trouble if I say that Jesus did not come to give us all the answers, or to fix our jobs or our marriages or our finances?

Is it possible that He didn't come to give me great success, or to help our football team to win, or even to make your church grow?

Is it just totally preposterous to think that He didn't come to lower taxes, to take over politics, or to fill the Supreme Court with conservatives or liberals?

Could it be that He didn't even come to "bless America," or that He is not necessarily an American at all?

What if He is really bigger than all of this, and that maybe we might do better if we just bow before Him in worship and submission?

What if we exist for Him, rather than Him existing for us?

What will happen if we just start all over, and this time *He* gets to be Lord and to do what *He* wants?

I know that's a crazy thought. Excuse me... I don't know what I was thinking.

21

Facing the Facts on a Fishing Trip

"The entire crew cheered and applauded. Everybody was smiling and laughing. Everybody but me."

My wife and I were taking a short vacation in Destin, Florida, and the emerald waters of the Gulf of Mexico enticed us to want to go deep-sea fishing. We got up that morning at four to depart from shore at five for a day-long fishing trip on a commercial party boat. Thirty other turistas joined us as we all joyfully headed into the deep waters of the gulf at sunrise with dreams of catching a big one.

My Type-A personality really shows whenever I go fishing. I work so extremely hard to try to catch everything I can as if my very life depended on it. After a few hours I am always the dirtiest, slimiest, bloodiest person on the boat! People learn to stay out of my way. This wouldn't be so ridiculous if I was good at it, but I am not. By mid-day I had a string of small snapper and a few other odd fish. I was still working in hopes of landing at least one fish that was larger than three pounds.

I'll never forget what happened next on that beautiful day. A young lady who was on the boat with us, in contrast to the rest of us, wore a nice dress with a matching white hat and white gloves. She enjoyed the ride on the boat but didn't fish at all, simply exclaiming, "I don't want to mess up my nails that I just had done!"

I rolled my eyes and thought to myself, "Oh brother! Why in the world did she come on this all-day-long fishing adventure if she didn't want to fish?" It was the most absurd thing I had seen on the entire trip.

A little later I heard her soft feminine voice say, "Well, I guess I need to fish a little bit. I just hope I don't get my nails dirty." I laughed to myself as I pulled in a one-pound snapper. "She will never catch anything! What a joke!"

Within just a few minutes, however, I heard a loud squeal from where the lady was fishing. My jaw dropped as I actually saw her pull in a huge, beautiful forty-pound grouper! It was the biggest fish anybody caught that day and much larger than any fish I had ever caught in my life! The lady was thrilled beyond belief. The entire crew cheered and applauded. Her nails and her clothes were still clean. Everybody was smiling and laughing.

Everybody but me.

From the moment I saw that grouper I began to develop what some people call a "slow burn." I continued to fish for a short while, but jealousy and resentment gradually took over my attitude until it showed on my face. I was no longer having fun. My wife could see it, and wisely said not a word.

Snatching the rod and reel from the water, I walked away

and stumbled up to the sundeck of the boat. Looking up into the sky, bitter and bloody and exhausted, I shouted angrily into the heavens. "WHY? WHY? WHY!! God, you KNOW I work so hard to catch fish, and you have NEVER let me catch a fish like that! And this girl didn't even try, and you gave her a bigger fish than I have ever had! WHY?"

I think that getting some kind of an answer from God has very little to do with the piety of our lives, but much to do with how desperate we are to hear. Such was the case that day on the boat. I didn't like the answer at first — actually I hated it. But in the midst of my selfish demand for an answer, I know what I heard. What I heard was... laughter!

Across the blue Florida skies, coming straight to my heart, when I asked for God to explain his reasons for not giving me the big fish, my only answer had been a hearty laugh! By that, I knew that He was saying, "It's my ocean, son, and they are my fish. I can do what I want with them, and you'll just have to deal with it."

No matter how much I cursed the whole situation and spit in the ocean and kicked the boat, He was, of course, right. I could complain that it just wasn't fair, and I could pout and say that I would never go fishing again. That would really show Him! But in the end I had to learn to deal with it.

Looking back now I realize that I learned two valuable lessons that day. Both of them are clearly taught in Scripture, but learning it from the Book and learning it from life are not always the same.

The first lesson was the truth of Matthew Chapter twenty, where the owner of a farm decided to pay the same amount to those who worked for one hour as he paid to those who worked all day long. Essentially, he said, "I can do what I want to with what is mine, and you don't get a vote." It is a lesson in sovereignty. He owns it and runs it, and I don't. There is only one God, and I'm not it. Being God, He can give his big fish to a young lady and not to me, if that's what he wants to do.

The other lesson is the truth of the elder brother of the prodigal son in Luke 15. On the boat that day, I was just like him. He had worked so hard for so long. He had done all the right things. When his wayward, undeserving brother got a big "welcome home" party, he resented it, and instead of enjoying the party he stood outside with a scowl. If he had been on a boat, he would have retreated to the sun deck! The fact that he had never been honored with a big celebration just ate him up. "*Why* him, and not *me?*" But the Father rejoices at the return of the prodigal!

This great story, of course, is a beautiful lesson of grace; a grace that could not be the reward of hard work, but is a great and wonderful *gift* to the undeserving, the unqualified, the unrighteous, who know that they could never ever pay for it unless it was absolutely free.

I still wish that I had been the one to pull in the big one that day. But if I had, I would probably be boasting about what a great fisherman I am. I'm sure that He knew best, and would rather that I learn these lessons instead of catching a huge grouper.

But, Lord, isn't there some way I could have learned this stuff and still got the fish too? (I think I might hear more laughter.)

As the little song goes, "He's got the whole world in His hands."

That includes the oceans, and the fishes, and you, and me.

22

Forgiveness In My Family

"It was still raining as my father quietly stepped inside, took off his coat and hat, and closed his umbrella. He stood in the doorway, not moving. Looking across the room at my mother, he spoke very softly."

My father grew up in an impoverished area in northern Alabama, and he used to tell me a lot of stories about his childhood. None of his family had ever finished high school. All of them knew a lot about how to work and somehow get by on a few potatoes and not much else.

Part of their culture was to escape their misery by finding a cheap way to get drunk on alcohol. Dad struggled to get away from that. When he was old enough to get a job in the city and away from the coal mines, that is just what he did. He got a job as a hospital security guard where he met a switchboard operator, fell in love, and got married at the age of twenty-two.

He joined the U.S. Army shortly after I was born, and

after his discharge from the Army he got a job in the steel mills of Birmingham where he worked for forty-two years. He was so proud to have this job. I remember him showing me one of his first "paycheck stubs" and the amount of take-home pay he earned for two weeks' work. He had made a total of twenty-one dollars.

But growing up as a small boy in Birmingham, son of a steelworker and a "full-time" mother, life did not seem bad at all. Of course, we had very little money. There were four of us boys, and I think I was nine when our family got its first automobile, a used-up 1948 Plymouth that had been a taxicab. Later in this book is a story about that car.

We fought over the "good" groceries early in the month, but toward the end of the month until payday when even the Spam was gone, we ate butter beans and potatoes, and for meat there was something called beef tripe. If you don't know what that is, you don't want to know! But life then was really not so bad. Dad was doing all he could to provide for us faithfully. We never missed air conditioning or television, because we had never had them.

Many fond family memories, however, are clouded by a dark shadow that hung over our household. It was never spoken of, but it was there. I didn't know what it was or what had caused it, until one time when my father drank too much. Suddenly I saw a twisted agony on his face as he sank to the floor in the corner of our living room. He began to cry and to scream words that came as an unforgettable shock to my little ears. "I'm going to kill him! I'm going to kill him! Oh God, please let me kill him!"

"Kill who, Daddy?" I asked. Everything got quiet, my mother pulled me away, and I was left to wonder what this was all about.

This kind of thing would happen again occasionally, maybe once or twice a year.

One night, when I was still a small child, my parents finally told me about something that had happened back before I was born. At the time, my father had a brother named Terry, less than two years older than he was. They were very close.

But then, on one awful day when my father was only sixteen, somebody came running up to him and said, "If you ever want to see your brother alive again, you better run down to the café!"

When my dad ran inside, Terry was lying on the floor dead. He had been carelessly murdered by a man he didn't know and never even saw. Terry had been eating a sandwich at the lunch counter and was stabbed in the back by a man who was showing off his new knife.

Of course, my dad's heart had been broken, and for many years now my sweet, gentle and hard-working father had carried a lot of anger, and when he dreamed, he dreamed of revenge.

Though this was always on my father's mind, we never discussed or even mentioned this horrible event. But one time I did ask him the name of the man who had murdered Terry, and I will never forget the icy cold tone of voice that he had when for the only time in his life I heard him speak this man's name.

Dad constantly harbored thoughts of even committing a crime just to get in prison to get at the man who had taken his brother's life. He tried to keep it all inside, and it was slowly destroying him. He learned not to open up, not to show his emotions, not to talk about his pain. Stomach ulcers, caused and aggravated by these suppressed feelings, were a constant problem to him, sometimes even sending him to the hospital.

Anger and bitterness were taking a heavy toll on this man I knew as "Daddy." Though I was just a boy, I could see he was hurting a lot, and I was helpless to do anything about it.

Several years passed, and things stayed about the same, until one day something happened that turned everything around.

It was a cold and rainy Sunday, and we had all gone to church that morning. When we returned home, my father wasn't with us. It rained heavily all that afternoon, and my brothers and my mother and I stayed inside, but he was gone.

I didn't know where Dad was or when he would be back. Then, sometime around four o'clock that afternoon, we heard the front door open.

It was still raining as my father quietly stepped inside, took off his coat and hat, and closed his umbrella. He stood in the doorway, not moving.

Looking across the room at my mother, he spoke very softly. Tears were in his eyes. A look of peacefulness was on his face. With a trembling voice he began to cry as he spoke.

"Kate, I'm free! I'm *free!*"

What had happened was that my father had spent the afternoon with the church pastor. He had poured out his heart to God, and had finally, after twenty long years, forgiven the man who killed his brother! For over half of his life, my father had let what that man had done rob him of rest, plague him with bitterness, destroy his nerves, and ulcerate his stomach. Now, he had finally put it behind him.

Later he explained to me that, as the pastor had told him, forgiveness doesn't mean you approve of, nor do you agree with, a wrong that was done.

It doesn't mean that wrong is right.

It doesn't mean that it doesn't still hurt.

It just means you decide to turn it loose, so it can turn you loose. Dad had finally, simply, let it go. At long last he was free — free to love, to laugh, to enjoy his family, to get on with this wonderful gift that we call life. After that, my father lived nearly thirty more years.

What I am hoping to relate to you in this story is this simple but profound truth: when my father was angry and bitter, he was not hurting the man who had killed his brother. That man was in prison somewhere, totally unaware of what my father was thinking or feeling. No, my father was only hurting himself and those of us who loved him. And when he forgave, it was *himself* who was set free!

The most tragic thing is not what someone says or does to hurt us, as bad as that might be. But the worse thing is what we do to hurt ourselves when we don't forgive.

Have you ever heard somebody say something like, "I will never forget what she said to me?" How long did it take for her to say it? Maybe four seconds? And, yet, we remember it for days, or months, or years, before finally we see how warped that is.

Forgiveness is required of all of us if we are to keep any sanity at all.

When we are honest about it, we know that we ourselves are often in the wrong and need to be forgiven by God and by others. Likewise, we all have also been hurt by somebody. Maybe it was careless or unintentional. Or maybe it was deliberate and mean. It doesn't matter. He commands that we forgive others who have wronged us. And He commands this, not just for them, but for *us*, so that *we* can be free.

129

The thought occurs to me that since God has indeed forgiven me for all that I have done, and since my father could forgive the man who had hurt him so much, I should have no problem forgiving anybody who ever hurt me– anybody, any time, anywhere, in any way.

One more thought. If you do forgive... or if you don't... you don't even have to say anything. Your children will know.

23

Free From Religious Performance

"Either we are actually free, free to do right or wrong, free to obey or to disobey, or we are not free at all."

After many frustrating years of "trying to be a good Christian," I finally did the most reasonable and sane thing that a human being can do.

I gave up.

Somehow we have turned what should be a joyfully liberating faith into a pressure-filled performance trap, and I fell into it. Finally, after so much effort, so many setbacks, and so much hypocrisy (my own) I decided to do myself and everybody else a huge favor: I just quit.

I wouldn't be honest if I told you that I never get religious any more. I still have returned to the struggle at times, re-entered prisons of my own making and played the silly games that people who want to be "good Christians" play. But I don't enjoy the games any more, and I don't stay very long in the prisons before I miss the fresh air of freedom.

Freedom is a beautiful word, and a beautiful feeling, and a beautiful experience! I would rather be free than to be rich, or smart, or good, or religious. I would rather be free than famous or successful. I am at a loss to express how important and how valuable it is to me.

Okay, try this one: it is better than being in love.

Well... close, anyhow.

The freedom of which I speak is not rebellious or defiant or angry. It is simply knowing what I am and what I'm not, knowing what I can do and what I can't do, knowing that my relationship with God is based on grace and acceptance rather than on my attempts to perform the impossible. Amazing grace; how sweet the sound!

Like many sincere people, I used to go to a lot of semnars and conferences. I loaded up my car with books and tapes, trying to find the key to a victorious life, an effective ministry, a happy marriage, and so on and on. I attended conferences on the deeper life, church growth, the Christian home, end time prophecy, soul-winning evangelism, prayer and fasting (I hated that one!), finances and family, substance and style, preaching and planning, holiness and healing, sex and stress (I'm not kidding) and more.

Christian "experts" in their chosen fields told us all the rules to follow to be a great success as a really great Christian. It was enough to make you either throw up or go crazy, and I think I did both!

Then in 1998 I was preparing to go to another one. This one, called "Born Free," was to be held in a huge church somewhere in the Atlanta area. On the way there my wife and I had a big argument in the car. You know, the usual thing about how she thought I was supposed to ask directions, when I *knew* that I could find it if I only drove around long enough!

We arrived late, upset and still a little angry. Finding my seat, I began to listen to the speaker, a well-known author and teacher named Steve Brown.

During the first few minutes I heard Mr. Brown say something like this: "If you are trying to get everything right about God and the ministry, you won't find it here."

That surprised me quite a bit. He went on to say that he didn't have many answers and didn't know anybody who did!

He said that he himself really messed up a lot, and that we will too, and that it was okay! He said that we didn't have to always be right or in control. He said that even sin and failure can be our friends!

Mr. Brown went on to say that he was probably wrong about half of the time, but he didn't know which half! He said that God was doing fine before we came along, and He will be doing fine long after we're gone. He said that God doesn't really need us, but He really likes for us to come to Him, messed up as we are — not so that He can fix us, but just so that He can love us!

He even said that when we really blow it, God is neither surprised nor angry. Finally, he said that there was nothing good that we could do to make Him love us more, and nothing bad that we could do that would make Him love us less!

Imagine what was going through my mind as I heard these words! Could it really be true?

Yes, instantly, I knew that it was!

For years I had secretly believed that something like what Mr. Brown said could be true, but nobody had ever told it to me without reservations and warnings which served to keep us in line. These reservations and warnings ruined the whole thing. There is no such thing as "freedom, but..." Either we are actually free, free to do right or wrong, free to obey or to disobey, or we are not free at all. Jesus said that we are "free indeed." I think He meant it! He went to a lot of trouble to secure this freedom for us.

Some well-meaning Christians will tell you that this teaching is dangerous — that it invites sin, and that it can get out of hand and you will go too far. Yeah, maybe so. But since nobody else, either inside or outside the church, can give you real freedom, you will soon come running back to the only One who can.

Becoming free has really made some strange changes in my life since we made that trip to Atlanta so many years ago. I can get drunk; I can cheat; I can do all kinds of immoral things. I can quit church altogether, and I can indulge in drugs, porn, or you name it.

But to say that I *can* do these things does not mean that I *must* do them. It doesn't take away the harmfulness of it.

And, surprisingly, there is also an increasing desire to cooperate in making my life a more grace-full life. I find myself *wanting* to please the One who has set me free!

The "Born Free" seminar taught me "You will never get better until you know that you don't have to get better." Mr. Brown was right when he said, "Obedience will never ever produce freedom, but freedom will eventually produce obedience."

Some of the results of becoming free are really a lot of fun to me, and I love telling you about them:

I laugh more. I don't always have to be right. I don't have to be agreed with. I don't have to be admired as a "good Christian." I don't have to look good. I can be more honest and real.

I can admit my many faults and failings, and can even talk comfortably about some of my sins. Here and there I have talked about a few of them in this book. There are, of course, many more.

I will not give you a list of them!

Recently we were in a church service where we were invited to write our sins on a piece of paper and then come forward and nail the list to a cross. One of my granddaughters was there and asked me what I had written on my list.

I replied that they didn't give me enough paper!

My point is that I can "lighten up" and quit pretending, since I'm truly free. I don't need to protect my reputation, worry about what people think, or prove that I am the greatest. I think I am becoming less of a pain in the behind. My obsession with perfection is now dead. When it died, I buried it and laughed on its grave!

I also stopped going to all those conferences!

If you have become weary of trying to do it right like a "good Christian," I invite you to do what I did.

Give it up.

Quit.

Put your burden down and join me in an old spiritual song:

"Free at last, free at last! Thank God Almighty; I'm free at last!"

24

Grace Heals Racism from the Inside

"I was in Birmingham at the same time, and these events were happening less that two miles from the place where my Bible lay open on my desk."

Historians tell us that two of the most significant moral and spiritual events of this country were the freeing of slaves in the 1860s and the civil rights movement exactly a hundred years later.

We have the good fortune of living in a land where the oppression of other people is recognized as being wrong and unacceptable. And we have this because some brave leaders had the courage to stand against it until it was defeated.

Having been raised in the old Jim Crow South, racism was so much a part of my young life that it took years for me to notice how ugly it was and how demeaning it was for both black and white people. Some of my father's relatives even had membership in the KKK, and they tried to get him to join.

"Why didn't you?" I once asked him. He said that he "just didn't feel like it." It was the only answer he ever gave me.

I had a conversion experience when I was nineteen, after I had already finished high school and spent some time in the military. Within a month I entered a college for the purpose of learning the Bible and theology and ministry.

The college was in Birmingham, and the time was the mid-sixties. Our way of life was changing right before us, and there was much resistance. You know the sad story.

People who just wanted to be treated as equals were beaten bloody with billy clubs.

The police knocked them down with water from the fire hoses.

Trained German Shepherds mercilessly attacked helpless people.

Many who had done no wrong except stand up for their own dignity were put in jail.

And one Sunday morning on Sixteenth Street, four little girls went to Sunday school and never came back alive because of a bomb that had been planted in their church.

Looking back at those times, I wish so much that I had been different. I would like to be able to say that I had been there, standing with my brothers as they marched against oppression and inequality. I wish that I had sung with them, encouraged them, and suffered with them. It would be nice to know that I had at least spoken up to try to stop the hatred and the violence.

After all, I was in Birmingham at the same time, and these

events were happening less than two miles away from the place where my Bible lay open on my desk.

There is no question in my mind that, considering where I was and what I knew, I was sincerely trying to learn the ways of the Lord. More than ever in my life, I had become focused on wanting to do the right thing.

But I did *not* stand up, and I don't personally know anybody who did. Not one of our teachers or "ministers of the Word" had anything to say, except to tell us to "stay out of it," "mind our own business," and to have nothing to do with these "agitators" who had come to our city.

According to popular opinion at the time, the policemen with their dogs and clubs and fire hoses were not the agitators. The angry racists throwing rocks and setting bombs were not the agitators. The people who simply wanted equal treatment under the law were the ones who were called agitators. Why, they were doing such terrible things! They wanted to sit at the same lunch counters, drink from the same fountains, sit wherever they could find a seat on a public bus, and to be able to vote. How horrible they were!

So our Christian ministers told us to stay away from such "troublemakers."

I find it strange that I never felt guilty about my non-involvement in this conflict. As years went by, elements of racism continued to be a part of my life, even as I preached sermons and did church work. I sincerely prayed and worked and served, but I never realized how hypocritical my life was.

One of the tragedies of human nature is that when we are part of a subculture that thinks a certain way, all of reality is defined within that subculture. Even our conscience can be bent to fit the accepted pattern of thought.

Fast-forward (please!) to a single day when I bought two books that soon changed my entire way of thinking forever!

Little did I know how graceless my soul had been until that day. The two books were not actually books about racism or social issues at all. They were books about the grace of God. One was "The Ragamuffin Gospel" by Brennan Manning. The other book was "What's So Amazing about Grace?" by Philip Yancey.

I promise you that I did not enjoy the books when I first read them. I cried like a baby through every chapter.

For the first time in my life, I was beginning to see what grace was really about — how extreme, unreasonable, radical, and wonderful it is!

Reading those two books, I finally saw the truth of how undeserving I was, and am, and always shall be. All of my pride, any sense of worthiness or righteousness of my own was obliterated forever. I saw myself as so much worse than I had ever imagined that I was, and, at the same time, I realized that somehow I was loved completely and unconditionally.

I thought upon the truths of radical amazing grace. I found out that even beginning to think upon the truths of grace can lead your mind into areas you have never visited before. You will see things differently, and you will hear a different voice speaking to you.

I began to think back on the years when we white Americans felt some sense of superiority, and it sickened me. It literally made me physically ill. Disgusted and ashamed, I prayed for and found forgiveness.

I know that I cannot go back to being the nineteen-year-old in that Bible College. I can't go back to the Birmingham of the sixties and try to make a difference. But I can look around me now, and ask for insight into my world today, hoping to not be so blind any more. And perhaps I can find some courage to do something about it.

Not long ago, I participated in a march to honor those who back in the sixties had stood for grace, non-violence, and freedom from oppression.

The newspapers reported that I was there to "atone" for my past. They were wrong. I can't atone for anything!

But I can be a different kind of man... if only because of grace.

25

Highways and Hedges

"A divine voice is calling us into the suburban subdivisions and the grimy ghettos, into the board rooms and the bar rooms, into every life wherever grace can reach, which is indeed into every life."

Two words that are often used by the emerging and emergent churches these days are "missional" and "incarnational." They are still new enough that my spell-check on this computer does not recognize the words and therefore underlines them in red. But they represent two good concepts. As I understand them, these are basically words that mean that Christians are to be missionaries in the world outside of the church walls and that we are to be an illustration and example of Christ through the way we live our lives in a down-to-earth way.

That is, we should get muddy and bloody by living as Jesus lived in the real world, not separated or isolated from sin and sinners.

Recently my brother Joe came down from Birmingham to visit with us for the weekend. At the time, our aged mother was staying in a nursing home recuperating from hip surgery. When I got out of church that Sunday, I called him to ask how he was and what he had been doing.

He said, "I went and saw Mom and took her for a ride to see the ducks and the birds and flowers, then got her some lunch, gave her a little tour around town, then took her back to the nursing home."

Facetiously, I responded, "Well, while you were out doing all of those Christian things, I was in church!"

We are living in a wonderful time when those of us who attend church are waking up to the truth that our service to God is not to be limited to what we do in and for our church, that the true test of our religion is what we do for poor and lonely and hungry and suffering people wherever we can help them.

I will even go so far as to say that it is better to do these things and not attend church than to attend church and not do these things!

Even today some churches seem to exist only for their own self-preservation. Spirituality is defined as being faithful to attend all the services, support the building program, pay the minister, sing in the choir, and so on. Other people who don't subscribe to these precise interpretations are considered to be "outsiders" who must be convinced to think exactly the way the insiders think. Ministerial success is defined by how many people they can get to assemble together. "Full-time Christian service" means church work, and you must be either a preacher or a music director or a youth minister or an evangelist for the church. Whatever else you do to serve God through your work or in your community is not really considered much of a ministry at all. It certainly is not worth mentioning in church if it isn't directly linked to the programs of the church.

In my opinion this is idolatrous, silly, and also very sad.

Let me be honest enough to confess to you that sometimes in my own life I still find it easier to do the stuff that we do inside the church walls, and harder to go to the uncomfortable places.

Doing "church work" is much safer than actually doing the true work of the church. But I am definitely changing. I just don't want to be smug in my criticism since I was at one time part of the problem.

But, as I said, this is a wonderful time, because many who so long have slept safely in their pews are now waking up! A better way is emerging — one that is more realistic, more unselfish, more helpful, and (I believe) more Christian.

I will share just a few examples:

Recently my son called me on a Sunday afternoon. "Dad, our church did something this morning that blew me away!" He then told of how the church had given every person an envelope, and in each envelope there was cash — anywhere from twenty to a hundred dollars. The leaders then told them to use this money to help someone in need. "It must be someone outside of your own family," they added, "and do *not* put the money back into the church!"

Well, that blew me away too! It does not matter that this particular church is not of my denomination. They have set a great example for all of us by teaching all of their people that everyone of them can be used to bless other people. This same church also gives away over a thousand bicycles to poor children at Christmas.

Another church in my town is building a medical clinic for those who can't afford the prices at the hospitals and doctor's offices. Patients are charged only what they can afford to pay, if anything. Generous and unselfish doctors (yes, there are some!) either discount or donate their services to help make it happen. What an awesome project and a great ministry this can be!

Many of our churches (including where I attend) are involved in caring for the displaced families and homeless people of our area, and putting them up in the church's facilities from time to time. Once a month we provide the best hamburgers you ever tasted for men from the half-way house, sharing a meal and ministry and fellowship with these, our friends, who were just released from jail.

A church in Birmingham has had forty of their families sell their homes and move into the inner-city area for the purpose of living their lives among the poor!

The greatest and most radical example of this that I have ever heard of is Shane Claiborne of Philadelphia. He and several young couples just out of college have given up their desires for a lucrative career and chosen instead to live homeless lives in the ghetto. In his book "The Irresistible Revolution" he tells of people who come in as tourists from churches to observe what he is doing.

When the church folks ask what is their "outreach program," Shane answers, "It's amazing! You guys just keep coming in here!"

(Think about it.)

I'm sure there are many other examples in your town and mine where people from church are climbing out from those pews and pulpits to enter the world where they are called to tell and to show the love of God. A divine voice is calling us into the suburban subdivisions and the grimy ghettos, into the board rooms and the bar rooms, into every life wherever His grace can reach, which is, indeed, into every life. Nobody is too good, and nobody is too bad to be included.

When we finally get to wherever we have been sent, we will find that He has been waiting for us. He was already there.

It has been more than half a century since, as a child, I sang this song in Sunday school, but it goes, "In the highways, and the hedges, I'll be somewhere a-listenin' for my Lord!"

I liked the song then, but I need it more now. And I really hope to see you somewhere in the highways and the hedges.

26

His Name Was Billy

"In that dark street, as Billy lay bleeding, he gurgled through his severed jugular vein a desperate prayer."

The year was 1974, in the city of Columbus, Georgia. The weather was hot. It was late on a Saturday night (actually early on a Sunday morning) and most people in Columbus were either working a weekend graveyard shift at the mills or had gone to bed.

But down in the heart of the city, in a dark neighborhood, a teenage boy named Billy was, as we say, "up to no good" at the time.

I am aware that it is not unusual for any of us, especially during teenage years, to get ourselves into trouble that turns out to be painful, shameful, and embarrassing. Fortunately, most of us find some way to survive those times and escape the most serious consequences of our actions.

Unfortunately for Billy, he got into deeper trouble than he

could handle, and the consequences were huge, and he did not escape.

In the fall of that same year, I was called to become the pastor of a little church in that same city. It wasn't long after I arrived that I met Billy's parents and heard his story. From what I was told, here is what had happened to him on that hot night in Columbus.

Billy and a friend were in his car, and they picked up a couple who directed them to stop at a particular house. Then Billy went into the house with the woman, thinking she was a prostitute, not knowing that he had been set up for a violent robbery.

He had walked into the wrong place at the wrong time, and a man with a big knife followed him into the house. He slashed and swung the knife at Billy. He stabbed Billy's chest just one-eighth of an inch below his heart. He then slit Billy's throat, completely severing his jugular vein. Then, with the third blow, he stabbed the knife into Billy's stomach, puncturing his liver. Billy staggered into the street and fell to the pavement in a huge pool of his own blood. The perpetrators ran the other way as Billy was left to die in the street.

In that dark street, as Billy lay bleeding, he gurgled through his severed jugular vein, a desperate prayer:

"Dear God, I am so sorry! My life for myself is over. I don't want to die like this! If you will *please* save me... save my life... I will live it only for you... and I promise I will never be ashamed of you!"

Just a block away was the largest hospital in Columbus. Billy was taken to the emergency room by his friend who had been waiting in the car. Billy was placed on a gurney and lay there bleeding as he heard this conversation:

"Call the coroner; this boy has been stabbed to death!"

"But I think he is still alive!"

"Yes, but by the time the coroner gets here, he will be dead. There's nothing we can do for this one."

[Before I go further into this story, let me say that I have heard so much hype and so much overstating, that I lean toward understating. I am reluctant to call something a miracle. I do not go around saying "God showed me this," and "God told me that." Having seen too much of it on television and in the pulpits, I do not wish to sensationalize anything. What I am about to tell you will sound that way, but this is as it really happened. For myself, I can only attribute it to being a miracle of God!]

One of Columbus' leading surgeons was home in his bed, sleeping. At the same time that Billy was being stabbed, he was awakened and felt that someone was saying to him, "Get up, *now*, and hurry to the emergency room!" This surgeon rushed in to the hospital, ran up to the place where Billy lay, and immediately took charge. He yelled for the people to not just let the boy die, but to wheel him into surgery at once!

The surgery lasted throughout the rest of the morning hours and on into the late afternoon. When it was over, Billy was still clinging to life. He spent several weeks in the hospital before finally coming home.

When at last Billy did come home, he was a different person. Physically, of course, he had scars on his chest and his neck. He was the only person from that hospital who had ever survived after having his jugular vein entirely severed.

But more than that, he was a different person spiritually. He remembered the promise he had made to God, and he kept it.

When I came to pastor that little church in October of 1974, it was kind of a messed-up church, and I was kind of a messed-up pastor. I wanted to serve the Lord, but I had an ego the size of the state of Montana. In my efforts to make it into a big church, I hurt a lot of people and made some enemies who, in turn, hurt me. I made many well-intentioned mistakes, and it finally blew up, and I left the church after only one year, starting another church across town. I am not very proud of those days.

But there was a young man back in the tenth pew of that little church that came to every service, intently listened to every word, and soon started following me around like a puppy.

He was only eighteen, but he was humble, he was genuine, and he was wise. Most of all, he was broken. He had been through hell. He wanted to know the Bible, and he loved God with a passion. He had scars on his chest and neck.

His name was Billy.

For the next several years he worked with me and helped me and asked a thousand questions. He began to tell his story in jails and youth meetings. He led our youth and prayed for people and studied his Bible and often preached.

After several years he began to notice my beautiful and sweet step-daughter, and before he ever asked *her*, he asked *me* if he could marry her! By that time I knew what an amazing man he was, and I was honored to say, "Yes, if it's okay with her!" They have now had a strong marriage and a growing family for nearly thirty years.

This would be quite a nice story if it all ended here, but it doesn't. The ministry of Bill Purvis was just beginning.

In the same city and in the same church where he served

as youth minister with me, he later came back to be the pastor.

Just about five miles up the road from where he was stabbed stands the largest church in Columbus. Thousands now attend the church where Bill Purvis has been the pastor for more than twenty-five years. Cascade Hills Church is filled with people with many dramatic stories... but probably none are more dramatic than that of their pastor.

But even with the blessings of great success, he has a gentleness, an authenticity, and a humility that you cannot miss. He has never tried to become one of those "big shot" preachers.

(You know what I mean... the ones with an ego the size of Montana... like I thought I wanted to be back in the seventies.)

Bill Purvis is a man who has never forgotten where he could be... and where he would be... without a miracle of God.

He is a man who by all normal human accounting would certainly have died long ago... just a teenager who was "up to no good..." bleeding on the streets... on a hot night in Columbus, Georgia... in 1974.

27

I Am Chosen

"Today when I hear somebody say, 'Look at those little kids, just playing ball without a care in the world,' I will reply something like, 'That's what you think! Sometimes being an eight-year-old can be hell.'"

When I was a kid in school, I was pretty smart for my age. One day the principal and my teacher contacted my parents and suggested that I be moved up a grade in school. They called it being "double-promoted." My parents seemed to be proud of this opportunity, and, hey... I was just a kid, so I went along with it, of course.

Little did I know that there was a huge downside to skipping a grade in school. Suddenly, I was an eight-year-old in a class full of nine-year-olds. When you're that age, a year makes a huge difference in your physical size and ability. When you're a boy, your self-worth is linked to who you could beat in a fight. I remember occasionally being slapped around or pushed out of the way, but that didn't seem to bother me much. What really hurt was when we had to choose up sides for any of the sports we played.

Whether it was baseball or football or kick-ball or dodge-ball, the scenario was always the same. I would be the last one that anybody wanted on their team. One of the first things I learned to do was to see how many boys were there. I always had to hope and pray for it to be an even number, not an odd number. If you've ever been in my situation, you know why that is. If the numbers are even, then even though you're the last one picked, you go to the team that had the second choice, because that gives you the same number of players on each team. What a relief it was when the numbers were even!

But the problem became a big deal when the number of boys was an odd number. I had to stand there helplessly, while this exchange went back and forth:

"You can take him!"

"No, we don't want him, you can have him!"

"No, it was your turn; you have to take him; we don't want him!"

Sometime this would go on for a minute or two, which seemed like forever to me. I wished that I could be somewhere else, anywhere else. I wanted so much to be chosen and not re-jected, but nobody would ever choose me.

I prayed that some little kid would come in to our class who would be a worse player than I was.

I even started intentionally making bad grades, in hopes that the teachers would put me back in the younger class.

Today when I hear somebody say, "Look at those little kids, just playing ball, without a care in the world," I will reply something like, "That's what *you* think! Sometimes being an eight-year- old can be hell."

One of the strongest desires that all of us humans have is the desire to belong... to be accepted... to feel like we fit in. If we don't have that, it really hurts a lot.

From those times on the ball field, I knew what it felt like to be humiliated and rejected, to think that I was unqualified and unacceptable. Fifty years later I can still vividly remember the pain.

Not only can I still remember the pain... I can still feel it. And from that time on, God only knows how many times my actions and my decisions have been motivated by fear of humiliation, fear of rejection, fear of being unacceptable. How many jobs I didn't apply for... how many dates I didn't ask for... how many opportunities when I was afraid to take the risk... because I couldn't stand the thought of being turned down, or of failing.

I don't think for a moment that this is uniquely my situation. I have met a lot of people in every situation of life, and probably the majority of them struggle, for some reason, with feelings of inadequacy, lack of confidence, or irrational fears.

And there are many for whom my example of not being wanted on the team may seem quite trivial when compared to the rejection they have had to live with.

I am not a psychologist, so I won't attempt to analyze this. But I have heard some experts say that even a baby in the womb can sense whether he or she is wanted by her parents. And there is not one of us who hasn't felt the wounds and the pain from some kind of emotional trauma in our past.

Recently, I went to church and heard the minister talk about something called "inner healing." He said that he had experienced it in his own life, and explained it like this:

He said that God is timeless, that God is outside of what we understand as time and is not limited by time, so He can step in to the past just as easily as He can step into the present or the future. The minister said that we could pray and invite the Lord to enter into that period in the past when we were hurt or lonely or afraid or rejected. We could ask Him to help us and heal us and comfort us.

Well, I thought about it and it seemed to have worked for the minister, and some others said that it also helped them. So I thought, "What could it hurt to try?"

Some very nice people prayed for me and with me, and we invited Jesus to go back to the playground of that old elementary school in Birmingham back in the fifties, and to enter that situation of long ago. We asked Him to find a certain little boy (me) that nobody wanted on their team. We asked Him to let that little boy know that He was there, and that everything would be okay.

I won't tell you that I saw flashes of light and heavenly visions and felt an earthquake in my soul. I didn't really feel much of anything.

But I left the place with a peaceful heart.

I can't brashly say that all of my feelings of inadequacy have miraculously disappeared, but I can say that what I needed to hear was what I heard:

"It's okay. Everything will be fine. I am here."

Somehow, that was enough.

I am not trying to get everybody to do this. I don't even know if it works for everybody. And inner healing, like any other good thing, can become the latest fad. I don't think God wants that. It is not a magic cure for all of our hurts. Some amount of pain is just part of our being human.

But something did change about my attitude as a result of this. And it was all I really needed.

It is the way that I choose to look at myself. And it goes something like this:

"I am not rejected. And I am not only accepted... I am chosen."

28

I Am Not Doing Fine

*"There is a pretty good riddle that goes, 'What is it
that you don't want to have, but if you do have it, you
don't want to lose it?'"*

It was January, which for some reason has never been one
of my favorite months.

I am really an optimist, and usually a cheerful person, but
January just doesn't sit well with me. Please excuse this some-
what negative beginning; I promise that it does get better at the
end. But in January there is always the "after-Christmas let-
down." The cold weather just takes its toll on my spirit, my
body becomes a pasty white, the phrase "back to the grind-
stone" seems appropriate, and my team never wins the Super
Bowl.

I never get excited about "January white sales..." does
anybody? Football is over, and baseball hasn't begun, and I
don't like basketball. I really miss the balmy winds and the

sunshine which are at least a part of every other season.

By mid-month I had blown all of my New Year's resolutions but one, which was to spend morning and evening carefully going through John Baillie's "Diary of Private Prayer."

Then something very traumatic happened that had the effect of distracting me to the point of breaking that last resolution.

There is a pretty good riddle that goes, "What is it that you don't want to have, but if you do have it, you don't want to lose it?" The answer is... a lawsuit. And for the only time in my life, in January, I found out that I had one. This was, of course, an extremely stressful situation, and it was taking a heavy toll on my emotions. I felt that I had been betrayed, personally attacked, and greatly misrepresented. For more than two weeks, each day became worse than the day before. It had gotten to the point that I couldn't sleep.

Months earlier I had been asked to speak at a banquet, and the date of the banquet came upon me right in the midst of this crisis.

Now, here I was, expected to speak to this crowd a message of humor, entertainment, and inspiration. But not one cell in my body had any inclination to be funny, entertaining, or inspiring.

What did I really feel like doing? I wanted to spit on somebody's furniture, kick my dog, and try out a few new curse words. (No, I would never kick my dog!)

On the way in to the banquet hall, several people greeted me with "How are you doing?" and I automatically said that I was fine. It was, of course, a lie.

After I was introduced, I stood in front of the people, and I didn't really want to be there. I had no idea of what to do next. Should I try to handle it like a trained monkey performing on cue? Should I attempt to be cool and professional, rather than to be transparent and vulnerable? Should I force a smile, tell a few jokes, and give out empty clichés about how I was "happy to be here tonight?" I tried, but the pain was too much, and within one minute I couldn't help but release my true feelings.

What came out was something like this:

"I know that I am supposed to stand up here like someone who has it all together, but, really, I don't! I don't have many answers at all tonight! I am confused, angry, frustrated and exhausted! I have lots of doubts about a lot of things. I am so worried and scared that it's hard for me to see straight. Right now I am just praying that I can hold it together without bursting into tears! Tonight somebody asked me how I was doing, and I said 'Fine.' It was not true — I'm not doing fine at all. To be honest, I am hurting so bad I can't stand it!"

The people in the audience gasped for a moment. Many grown men had their mouths wide open. Even though it was January, I'm sure that some ladies were reaching for their fans.

I looked down, feeling that I had greatly disappointed the entire audience. Surely they were all wishing that they had invited someone else to speak instead of me.

Then, when I finally looked up at the audience, I saw that their faces were looking at me with smiles of sympathy and understanding. Rather than judging or criticizing me, they felt compassion for me. One of the men began to cry into his handkerchief. They listened carefully to my words, nodded in agreement, and gently encouraged me with interjections like "That's right," "You're telling the truth, man," and "Amen."

After I finished my little talk, we all shared together about how sometimes life is tough and sometimes our problems seem so huge that we wonder if we will get through them. We commiserated on the feelings of depression that come, the paranoia that we feel when people oppose us, and how much we really need each other when the going gets really rough.

Amazingly, nobody mentioned that we should just "cheer up and praise the Lord!" They gave me hugs and words of appreciation for my honesty. Tears were in their eyes and mine.

Undoubtedly, rather than my ministering to them, these people were the ones who ministered to me that night. Some of the people from that banquet are friends of mine even to this day.

Wherever we go, we really need to be aware of the fact that many people around us have overwhelming pain in their lives at the very moment in which we encounter them. What a shame that we seldom notice and are not tuned in to pick up the signals that somebody's heart could be breaking right now.

It might be him, it might be her, it might be you, or it might be me.

We have become experts at hiding it when we shouldn't. Somebody asks "How are you doing?" and we so often answer that we are "fine," "great," or "wonderful." Sometimes it is just a cover-up, a gloss-over, a lie.

Now, I am not suggesting that you dump every little trouble you have onto everyone who greets you with "How are you?" That would make the U.S.A. into a very strange country indeed! But... when it hurts so bad that we can hardly stand it... we should try to find someone who cares, and open our hearts up to that person. It can be the beginning of healing, ministry, and deeper friendship.

I saw a sign in front of a church down the road from my

house. It said "If you are looking for a sign from God to go to church, this is it."

Sometimes we are waiting for God to do something "spooky," and He wants to use something ordinary.

Usually, when prayers are answered, God does not drop something from the sky. God does the answering, but He usually answers by putting *people* in the right place at the right time to do the right thing. But we can miss it if we polish our phony smiles and pretend that we are fine when we are not.

Not every time, but sometime, if someone asks how I am, I want stop everything and think about how things are really going. I want to take the time to look into their eyes and see if I can see something. Perhaps I am really hurting. Perhaps they really care.

Then also, sometime when I ask "How are you doing?" I hope someone will look at me to see if I care. I hope that they will find me to be concerned, compassionate, and non-judgmental.

When a really hurting person meets a really caring person, he or she should really tell the real truth. In so doing, an awesome God could be about to answer a desperate prayer!

So, really... how are you doing?

29

I Hope You Dance

"Here I was, the owner of a radio station. Believe me, it didn't take long for buyer's remorse to set in!"

Back in 1995 I felt strongly compelled to try to buy a radio station and turn it into a Christian ministry. I didn't have the money, but I still wanted to do it. As we sometimes say, it was really "on my heart" at the time. So I got a home-equity loan, sold my truck, borrowed a little from my mother, and finally scraped up enough for a down payment on a little country AM station. I also signed a ten-year note for just a few bucks short of three thousand dollars a month.

Looking back now, I laugh at how I brought a trunk-load of Gospel records into the studio to play.

Do you remember records, played on a turntable? I had never even touched a CD, much less a computer! Even in 1995, I was hopelessly out-of-date.

But here I was, "owner" of a radio station.

Believe me, it didn't take long for buyer's remorse to set in.

It dawned on me that the world was not just sitting there listening to the static, just waiting for my broadcast to begin! Quickly, I realized that most people were not "out there in radio-land" and didn't care the least bit whether I was on the air or not.

As we say in the South, I had bit off more than I could chew.

All alone in that little studio, over my head in debt, all of my doubts and fears surfaced.

"What if I have made a huge mistake? What if nobody will listen to a little Gospel station? What if I can't sell any advertising? What if I go bankrupt? What if I lose my house? What if we go broke and I can't pay this bill and my wife leaves and my dog starves and my friends say they don't know me and my grass grows up because I don't have gas for the lawn-mower and people say they knew all along I was a loser, and what if...?"

The "opportunity" I had jumped into had become a heavy weight on my shoulders. I wanted to turn back, but it was too late. I had signed the note and committed myself for a long long time to come. I hadn't even started, and already I regretted what I had done. What was I thinking?

Tears started rushing down my cheeks. Exhausted, confused, and terrified, I wept over my lost safety and security.

What happened next is something I shall never ever forget. I promise you, this is exactly what happened!

Even as I was crying, at that very moment, there came a knock on my door. There stood a man I had never seen before.

He asked me, "What is this place?"

I wiped my tears and told him it was a radio station.

This strange man paused, looked me in the eye, and said, "Sir, I don't know what you are trying to do, but as I was driving down the highway, a voice spoke to me in my car. I believe it was the voice of the Lord, telling me to turn around at once! So I turned around! I drove several miles. Then I had a strong impression to turn into your driveway and come to this building."

After pausing again, he continued.

"I am here to tell you, sir, that you have *not* made a mistake! You are in the right place. You are going to be blessed. And He will meet your every need... so please don't be afraid!"

He then said a prayer for me and drove away... not in a chariot of fire, but in his car.

Beginning then, and for five more years in that little radio station, those words were proven to be true. What a time we had there! We didn't get rich, but we had so much fun and excitement! We worked hard, learned a lot, and the broadcasting helped a lot of people.

And the payments were made on time, every time but once when I was six days late.

I use this little story to remind myself, and you too, that unusual things will happen to us only if we are willing to be in a position where the unusual is what we need. When we "stick our necks out," dramatic things can begin to take place.

Especially when we are attempting to do these things to help others, we may see a lot of what I call "divine coincidences," or "minor miracles." But they're not minor when they are happening to *you*!

I am not recommending to you that you immediately go do something impulsive and stupid. I'm not trying to mess up your life, but to awaken it. I'm here simply to say, "Follow your dreams, take the chance, break out of the rut, and attempt something special!"

Trust me — you may cry, you may get scared to death, and you might even fail. But in the end you will be glad that you made the effort.

The old proverb says, "Nothing ventured — nothing gained." But I think country singer Lee Ann Womack says it best:

"I hope you never fear those mountains in the distance,

Never settle for the path of least resistance,

Living might mean taking chances, but they're worth taking,

Loving might be a mistake, but it's worth making,

Don't let some hell-bent heart leave you bitter,

When you come close to selling out, reconsider,

Give the heavens above more than just a passing glance,

And when you get the chance to sit it out or dance,

I hope you dance!"

If you can hear the faint sound of music playing somewhere in your heart, listen! This might be your song.

Don't sit it out!

30

Jim, Tammy Faye, Larry King and You

"Somewhere around that time it occurred to me that I could be standing on holy ground!"

I saw the slow and agonizing decline of Tammy Faye, as many of you did. This once-beautiful lady slowly succumbed to the ravages of cancer, but even as her physical appearance declined, her spirit got stronger.

I was not a big fan, and Tammy would be the first to admit that she was comically flaky, but I never questioned her sincerity. So I watched the coverage that was given on television when it was announced that Tammy Faye Messner, Jim Bakker's former wife, had finally died.

What impressed me most was a re-run of an earlier broadcast of the Larry King TV show which I had never seen before.

Tammy had just done another interview on the show the week of her death, which showed how cancer had so horribly destroyed her body. But this particular program I am talking about had been from a couple of years back.

There on this show were Jim and Tammy, along with their son and their daughter. Tammy still looked healthy at the time. It had been recorded years after they had both remarried, after Jim had been released from prison, and several years after the PTL empire had fallen in what people call disgrace.

I watched and listened carefully as they discussed the shame, the scandals, the divorces, the new spouses, the imprisonment, the former drug habits and rebellion of their son Jay, and the cancer that was then just beginning to attack Tammy Faye.

Many would think, after all that had happened, that some of the people in this broken family would be on the defensive. I watched to see if anybody was cynical or bitter. I wondered if somebody would show anger, or if the Bakkers or the Messners or the children would blame someone else, or each other.

Amazingly, not once throughout the program did anyone hurl an accusation or try to place blame, or seek to justify themselves or their own actions! I saw no hatred. I heard no name-calling. Nobody showed disrespect to any other person. There were no pot-shots, no cynical comments, nothing said at all that might even have had an edge to it.

Larry King asked how Jim felt toward Tammy's husband Roe Messner. Jim smiled and said that he was a wonderful man and a dear friend, and he sincerely wished for them to be happy. The children (now young adults) echoed the sentiment.

Likewise, when Larry King asked Tammy Faye and the kids about Jim Bakker's current wife, they enthusiastically expressed a genuine admiration and respect, and warm affection for her.

Now I understand that it would be pretty hard to fool a seasoned interviewer such as Mr. King, but the Bakkers didn't try to fool anybody. They were genuinely open, honest, humble, peaceful, and kind.

Perhaps the tabloid writers would have been disappointed, but for the rest of us it was refreshingly sweet, wholesome, and even loving. You don't see that every day!

The program closed with King's sincere comments on what a wonderful family he thought they were and how much respect he had for all of them.

Somewhere around that time it occurred to me that I could be standing on holy ground!

In my imagination I began to think back to a time long ago... a time when perhaps a young Bible school couple must have talked together about their dream of a worldwide Christian program on television. I wondered if they had even envisioned a park, or hotels, or conferences. Undoubtedly, they had great hopes to succeed in their ventures, and, probably beyond their wildest expectations, they actually did!

Of course, it is obvious that they never thought they would fall as they did. It probably never occurred to them that they would fail morally and spiritually.

But somewhere along the way, they let the fame and the money and the success compromise their character, and it all came tumbling down... and the crash of it was heard all over the world.

I am sure that if they had known of all the things that would happen, they would never have "signed on for the trip."

No doubt there were times they would much rather have remained unknown than to become a long-running joke on the Tonight Show. I believe that the pain of their failures had for years outweighed the happiness of their successes.

As William Cowper wrote, God really does work "in mysterious ways, His wonders to perform!"

Something totally different, something Jim and Tammy never thought would happen, must have been on God's mind from the very beginning! And through all of it, He never stopped loving them, and was never taken by surprise at anything they did.

Does God *cause* people to sin? Of course not! But He is never perplexed as to what He intends to do about it, and He is never without a plan to make it work out for good.

I'm aware that there are many people who think that any Christian who fails is an embarrassment to the cause of the gospel.

If I were to agree with a person who believed that... well, we would both be wrong!

Some people just don't yet understand that it really is entirely a message of grace! It's not about our always doing it right, but about love and acceptance and forgiveness, about restoration and redemption after we have made a total wreck of our lives.

Concerning God's grace, the fact is that we don't even know what we are talking about until we have fallen hard enough and often enough that we are no longer shocked at the depth of our own sinfulness.

Religion without grace can only focus on the rules we must keep and the commands we must obey. It gives us a pat on the back and makes us feel good that *we* have never done anything "really bad" like some others have done. But the powerful reality of true grace shines brightest only when we see that we have sinned, and sinned greatly.

If you are one of the people who has "never done much wrong," I can only recommend an honest and humble look within. If you still see yourself as a really good person, you have permission to look down on the rest of us.

But if you have really sinned — if you have tumbled off the pedestal — if you have been to the wrong places, done the wrong things, and got caught before you got around to repenting...

If you have lost your temper, fallen off the wagon, or wrecked your marriage, or anything that made you feel so ashamed...

If you have repeatedly needed forgiveness, and even now you can't seem to get your life together without messing up something... well... welcome to the human race! And welcome to amazing grace! The kingdom of God was made for people like you!

Everybody doesn't "get it," but Jim and Tammy do. No, it wasn't in their plan... but it was in His.

31

Listen to Your Life

"He is not speaking through the whirlwind or the earthquake, but through the still, small voice."

A young man was standing over the crib of his newborn baby, intently staring. His wife tiptoed into the room and stood beside him, filled with joy as she looked upon their first child. She saw that her husband's face was filled with wonder and admiration. Tears were in her eyes, and her voice trembled with emotion as she put her arm around him and softly whispered, "A penny for your thoughts!" Truly this was one of those very special moments!

Then she heard his answer: " I was just thinking that, for the life of me, I don't see how they could make and sell a crib like that for just $79.95!"

We have designed and built a society that is full of time-saving gadgets, but we still cram our days so full of activities that we never stop to smell the petunias. If we aren't busy, we are bored. If we stop to really listen to somebody, or to hear the birds sing, or to contemplate what is true or meaningful in life, there is a little man down inside us saying to us that we need to get moving because we are wasting time.

Frederick Buechner, a favorite author of mine, will tell you that his main message is to "Listen to your life." All around us there are things happening that we somehow don't tune in to.

Buechner has me convinced that God primarily speaks to us through little incidental happenings and casual conversations, not through great prophetic utterances and dramatic events. In other words, He is not speaking through the whirlwind or the earthquake, but through the still, small voice.

Recently, after reading from one of his books, I just went outside and lay down on a blanket in my back yard. I was amazed at the sounds and the smells and the sights of birds and bugs and the gentle breeze! I couldn't help but think of how much I had missed! It had been a long time since I had gazed at the stars at night.

I have charged the battery on my cell phone, but I haven't often charged the battery of my soul. I often fill my gas tank for fifty dollars, but I too seldom fill my life with wonder for fifteen minutes.

I believe that if we develop a listening heart, we will find that Someone is speaking to us in many ways in our lives, possibly even every day.

When a friend gives you a warm greeting, or when a child brings you a picture that she colored, or when a sweet old dog licks your face, or when somebody calls your number "by mistake," or when you see someone with a broken-down car on the road... it just might be your moment to enjoy, to see, to hear, to learn, and to serve. We can't schedule certain times for it to happen, and we certainly can't choose the means by which a message will come to us.

But it will come to us... somewhere, somehow.

Biblical times relate that God spoke to people through dreams, storms, birds, fish, bushes, gourd plants, and even donkeys!

I have known people whose lives were changed for the better through a TV newscast, through a loss of a job, or through a car wreck. Many, including myself, have found a new perspective on life through a song on the radio, or the most unintentional casual comment from someone.

I don't know anybody who is an expert on this; I certainly am not. But I believe that we should always be listening for the still, small voice.

In my experience it has always been a surprising message at an unexpected time. It cannot be "worked up" or made to happen. It is not a means to authenticate or confirm my own selfish decisions to do what I want to do. Once I heard a comedian say that he prayed that if he was supposed to get a dozen Krispy-kreme donuts to just have an empty parking place waiting for him. He said, "Amazingly, there it was, just when I circled the block the eighth time!"

The possibilities are limitless. Something may speak to you through a book, a blue bird, or a bumper sticker. It could be a frog or a fish or a feather. Perhaps it will be a sunrise, a song, a smile, or a snake in your yard. We must be listening in order to hear.

We are told that "Every good gift comes from above." I believe that truth, wherever and however it is found, comes from the one Source of truth, who is much greater than my understanding, much larger than my life, and much bigger than my religion. When somebody helps us or is nice to us, or when we have an opportunity to help or be nice to someone else, we may someday find that it was divinely appointed.

The main thing is to keep listening to your life.

A great popular song from years ago said, "Every time I hear a newborn baby cry, or touch a leaf, or see the sky, then I know why; I believe."

I do believe, Lord! Please help me not to miss the baby by just looking at the crib.

32

Moonshine from the Jailhouse Parking Lot

"The police were humiliated and embarrassed that the stuff had been stolen from their own parking lot. Heads were going to roll!"

If it were not for grace, and the lessons that we learn as we grow up, the following story would be embarrassing for me to tell. But the youthful foolishness of it all is something that I need to remind myself about, at least occasionally.

When I was a teenager, I thought that it would make me cool if I hung out with the troublemakers in my high school. They got a lot of attention, even if it was negative attention. Paul talks about some people who "glory in their shame." That was us. We boasted and bragged about the wrong things we did. With them, I could be an underachiever and curse and gripe about everything, and I would fit right in. And if you remember being a teenager, you know that "fitting right in" with some kind of group was extremely important! So my friends were always in trouble, and often I was, too.

Actually, at first I made good grades in school. Then one day when we got our report cards, all the guys were bragging about how many Fs they made!

I looked at my report card and saw the good grades and knew that they would ask to see mine. At that time, we were walking past a small pond. So, with much flair, I said, "My report card is so bad I'm gonna feed it to the fish!" With that, I wadded the report card up and threw it in the water! It saved me from the peril of not fitting in with the guys who made Ds and Fs.

After that, I learned to deliberately give the wrong answers on all of the tests. Don't tell me how sick that was... I know.

Later, when I was trying to get into college, my bad grades almost kept me from being accepted. I was admitted on academic probation, but graduated with honors.

What insanity makes people go to such extremes? It is the emptiness of our souls that makes us want to be accepted and to belong, whatever the cost.

It was sometime in October of one of my high school years that most of my friends started stealing the hubcaps off of cars. Somehow I missed out on all of that "fun" and never got involved in it.

I will never forget laughing about it when two of my best friends, who were brothers, had the police come to their home looking for the culprits. Their father answered the door and said that his boys would never do anything like that, and then he began to show them through the house. When he opened their closet door, hubcaps came falling out of the closet and rolling across the floor!

Probably because of them, I don't think they make hub-caps any more.

After they were caught in this crime, the city of Fairfield, Alabama made an arrangement that these two, along with three other "friends" of mine, would continue in school during the week, but had to spend every weekend in jail. When they were home during the week, they would even talk about what a great time they were having in jail. I was lonely when they were gone, and even a little jealous of them, until one of them finally told me the truth... that it was absolutely miserable, and that being in jail was not fun and certainly not "cool." Still, my weekends were empty and boring with all of my buddies incarcerated.

It was during this time that something very unusual happened. (I'm not making this up!)

Three of these guys called me on a Sunday afternoon after their release from their weekend in jail, saying they needed my help. I thought to myself, "Wow! I'm really in with these guys now!"

Another inmate had told them that his car had been confiscated and was in the city parking lot, and that it had forty gallons of moonshine whiskey in it that the police hadn't found! He told them that they could have all of the moonshine if they would just get it out of his car before the police discovered it!

So they had sneaked into the police impound lot, taken the illegal whiskey from his car, hidden it in the alley behind the police station, and now they needed for *me* to come with my old Dodge and load it up and take them around so they could sell it to somebody and "make lots of money" with it.

I was thrilled at the opportunity to be involved in something so exciting, and so happy to this time be a part of what they were doing. I didn't even hesitate.

After going several places trying to sell the moonshine without success, we decided to divide it up and keep it. Each of us kept ten gallons. Of course, we all talked big about how we were going to drink it, but I was afraid to even taste it and I buried it in my back yard. A neighbor saw me digging the hole and called my father, who asked me about what I had buried and made me dig it up.

To say the least, my father was very upset with me, but together we quietly poured it down the bathtub drain. In one of the stupidest moments of my young life, I actually asked him if I could just have a little of it to see what it tasted like.

Dad almost lost his control when he heard those words from me. He hit the ceiling as he shouted, "Hell, no!"

It wasn't long before the police somehow found out about all of this, and the newspapers got the word, too. The police were humiliated and embarrassed that the stuff had been stolen from their own parking lot. It was all to come up at a specially-called town council meeting that very next night. It was the first time I ever heard the expression that "Heads were going to roll!"

I will never forget what my father did the night of that town meeting. Very sternly, he told me to sit in the house and to not go anywhere or talk to anybody. He said, "I'm going to the meeting. You stay here!"

Later I learned that the place was full of people, and many of them were shouting questions at the mayor and the chief of police. Some were ridiculing the situation. The city decided to lock up (full time) the other boys who were involved in this incident. Then someone shouted my name, and asked what they were going to do with me! Some others then started shouting my name and asking where I was, saying that maybe I should go to jail, too.

And that's when my father came through — big time!

He had only a tenth-grade education and a mild gentle manner. He certainly was no public speaker. But that night my dad was a ferocious lion as he stood up to these lawyers, policemen, newspaper reporters, and angry citizens! He told them that if they knew what was good for them they had better leave me alone! (I think he included a few more choice words along with this warning!)

Amazingly, they listened to him. My hide was spared, and my head didn't roll.

Some people, because of some pain or disappointment in their family background, always have difficulty referring to God as "Father." But not me. I didn't know it at the time, but I was seeing God in my dad that night! Yes, he was disappointed in me and hurt and probably pretty angry. But the bottom line was that he loved me so much that it scared those people!

No matter what I had done, he was ready and willing to protect me and defend me, not because I deserved it (I didn't); but because I was his child.

I don't remember his ever teaching me about grace and mercy and unconditional love. But he did even better. He showed it to me in his life.

If you can't see God in that, you must not be looking.

Thanks, Dad!

33

My Pity Party

"I was no longer reluctant to present to an awesome God all of my sinfulness, my foolishness, my nothing-ness. I knew that it was all I really ever had to offer, and it was okay."

Most people find me to be cheerful and optimistic, but sometimes I can get discouraged along the way. It doesn't happen very often, but when it does, I find it so hard to break out of the discouragement. Sometimes I get an attitude of bitterness and resentment, which is certainly not good. But if I will just somehow hang on, God may take those times and turn them into something beneficial. It happened to me recently.

The day was hot, but not nearly so hot as my friend's temper! It was one of those things where "he said that he said something and what I thought he said was not what he said he said, so he wanted me to meet him someplace other than where I thought he said, so he had to either wait or walk, and I thought everything was fine while he was getting really, really angry."

Don't try to follow that. It doesn't matter, except that it was a classic failure to communicate. As a result, it came as a total surprise to me when he just exploded! He was so upset by that time that all apologizing and all pleading and all attempts at reasoning with him just made everything worse.

He was fine the next day, and I said that I was fine, too.

But my spirit was wounded by the hurtful words, so much so that I felt the wounds deeply and found it difficult even to smile.

I hate it when things like that happen. We can say that things are all right and we know that in time they will be, and we don't want to add any more drama to the situation. But for now, our emotions are raw and our joy of living doesn't exactly come bouncing back with a celebration and a parade.

Then, only two days later, a person very close to me took that time to set aside all verbal restraints and decided to "let me have it" about something! I don't even remember what caused it, but my spirit went from very low to devastated. I wanted to cry and cuss and spit on a cat.

I began a litany of complaint to myself. "Nobody appreciates me. Nobody understands me. Nobody cares how I feel!"

I had reached the point to where my face had such a spiteful look that even my dog kept her distance. By that time, I didn't like anything or anybody! Yes, I was having a major "pity party."

I know all about pity parties, so if you want to know about them, listen up while the expert (me) speaks:

The worst thing about a pity party is that all the people

you want to attend it usually don't show up. They don't send presents, either!

You build the entire party around the fantasy that a lot of people are going to notice how hurt you are, and how hard you tried, and how misunderstood and persecuted you are. They won't notice.

You spend a lot of time daydreaming that suddenly everybody is going to come up and say, "You poor dear! You have to go through so much! We are so sorry that your feelings are hurt! Please forgive us! We finally realize how wrong we were, and what a wonderful person you are! Let us bring you some cake, and then we will rub your back!" They never do.

After a couple of days of waiting, the candles burn out, the ice cream melts, and you begin to realize that nobody is going to come up to you and sympathize with you. At most, they just notice that you are being cranky and have a stinking attitude. How little do they know or care how you've suffered.

I may be being a little sarcastic... but if you think I am exaggerating, I'm not!

Finally, after it was clear that nobody else was going to attend the party, I did an unusual thing. I invited God in on it.

I had been reluctant to invite God to my pity party, for reasons that seemed obvious to me. I just knew that He would ruin the whole thing and would tell me how childish I was and essentially would give me a stern rebuke. Finally, I invited Him anyway.

I cannot tell you how surprised I was at what happened next. I sensed very strongly that He just showed up and said:

"I am so glad to be here with you, even if it is a pity party! I am not the God of your past when everything was fine. I am

not the God of your future, waiting to be with you only after you straighten up your attitude. I am the God of right here and right now... and I am happy to be with you here at this very moment. I would very much like to stay with you for as long as you want me to."

Yes, for the past few days I had forgotten all about grace, had refused to be at peace, and had dismissed real love from my life. But now, in the presence of One who is infinitely kind, I quickly realized that my pity party could now be over!

I was no longer reluctant to present to an awesome God all of my sinfulness, my foolishness, my nothingness. I knew that it was all I really ever had to offer, and it was okay.

I picked up my copy of "Abba's Child" and let the book read me. Listening to some soft music, I meditated on how gentle and tender God had been to me.

I decided to work on changing my life in two specific ways. One thing I decided was to only be in one place at one time. [Really! How hard can that be?] I mean that when I am with somebody, I want to be with them one hundred percent. I want to live in the here and now, because it's the only place where I really live and exist.

The other thing I decided was to seek to always respond with gentleness and kindness. It is not my job to straighten everybody out, to pretend spiritual or intellectual superiority, to justify or vindicate or defend my own ego, or to criticize what I disagree with.

After all, I had been in the presence of someone who could have passed judgment on my silly little party. He could have ridiculed me, reminded me how ungrateful I was, and told me of my many sins. But, instead, He merely chose to attend! Right now I don't think I can get over that.

I hope that I never do.

34

Playing It Safe

"I know that there are spiders in the trees and snakes in the grass, and that if you go where you've never been before you might step in something."

I will admit to sometimes being more than a little eccentric. Once someone told me that I was "a weird dude" and I took it as a compliment. So if you read this and disagree with me, you at least have my thanks for reading it. By the way, nothing that I write is written with the expectation that everyone will agree with it. But please give it some thought before you dismiss it as an idiosyncratic rant:

We in America have reached a level of comfort for which we can be thankful, but I think we have taken it much too far. We have insulated and isolated ourselves to the point of being ridiculous. We seem to think that we ought to have a life that experiences no discomfort of any kind. This is not only impossible to attain, but I don't think that it's healthy for us spiritually or mentally.

Our modern houses are air-tight, energy-efficient cocoons with only a few windows, and those are double-paned. Our homes and our cars are climate-controlled so that we can always stay cool in the summer and warm in the winter.

Even when we go to the beach on our vacations, many only look at our view of the ocean. If we swim at all, it is in sanitary, temperature-controlled pools where the posted rules are to shower before you get in and shower when you come out. How nice it is, we think, to lie beside the pool and look at the ocean without experiencing sand in our toes or salt water in our eyes!

For communication, we have MySpace and Facebook and Twitter and text messaging. Or we may "chat" online with some "friends" that we have never seen nor met in person. This is really nice. You don't have to get dressed or comb your hair or travel any distance to see them!

And if you don't like the way the "conversation" is going, you don't even have to wave goodbye or smile or be nice. You just push a button and log off of the chat.

For entertainment, we look at a tube or a screen so we can watch other people called "actors" portraying fictional characters going through experiences that aren't really happening! Then many of us become obsessed with every detail of these actors' lives and fawn over them as celebrities. I promise you that there are many people who know more about the "Brangelina" family than they do about their next-door neighbors.

For sports, we watch the screen so that we can see our favorite golfer or NASCAR driver or our favorite team. We smother ourselves in statistics about them without ever personally hearing the crack of the bat or the music from the marching bands. Then we listen to the discussion and analysis of the games. Incidentally, these games are played by professional athletes that we have never met and do not know, or by students at a school which we never attended.

Stepping back and looking at this, it appears to be not only absurd, but actually quite sad.

So I have come up with a novel idea! Some will say it is too dangerous and shouldn't be tried. (Don't believe them; they are wrong!) Here's what I think we should do:

When it's summer, go outside and walk and listen to the bugs buzzing and the birds chirping. Smell the grasses... get dirt on your hands... and feel the hot wind on your face. Drive with the windows down and let it mess up your hair. Sweat a little bit. When you go to the beach, get out in the ocean. Get some of that beautiful sand in your toes, and taste some salt water in your mouth, and let the waves crash over your head. Get a little sunburn. (No tanning booths allowed!)

When you get home, open the windows and let in the fresh air. Let the poor dog come in the house for a while!

And the next time that it rains, do what I often do: go outside and lie down on the grass and get really wet. Or at least walk in the rain. You won't melt.

Then when winter comes, follow the same idea. Allow yourself to get a little bit cold. Feel the cold wind in your face. Let your ears and nose get numb from cold. Smell the odors and the aroma of the cold season. Listen to hear the noises and sounds of winter in the country and in the city.

I know that everybody says this, but when you are cold, you are not really "freezing," and when you are hot, you are not really "burning up." Also, when you are hungry, you are not "starving," and when you are afraid of something, it will probably be okay; you are not "scared to death!" All of these, of course, are just expressions that Americans use when we experience even the slightest discomfort.

Following this same way of thinking, is it such a radical idea that we might consider talking to more people face to face?

Could we, in sports, either get in the games ourselves, or at least *go* to the games in person, rather than just look at a screen and hear people talk about a game that is already over?

For entertainment, can't we work on building for ourselves a life, rather than vicariously following fictional adventures or the details of the lives of celebrities?

I'm just saying that life is to be lived adventurously by *us*, where we are, right now in this moment!

I came across a hilarious list of complaints and suggestions that park visitors had turned in to the staff at Bridgers Wilderness Park in Wyoming. Here they are:

(1) Trails need to be reconstructed. Please avoid building trails that go uphill.

(2) Too many bugs and leeches and spiders and spider webs. Please spray the wilderness to rid the area of these pests.

(3) Please pave the trails so they can be snow-plowed during the winter.

(4) Chairlifts need to be in some places so that we can get to these wonderful views without having to hike to them.

(5) The coyotes made too much noise last night and kept me awake. Please eradicate these annoying animals.

(6) A small deer came into my camp and stole my jar of pickles. Is there a way I can get reimbursed?

(7) Escalators would help on the steep sections.

(8) It would be nice to have a McDonalds at the trail head.

(9) Too many rocks in the mountains.

When Moses went up to the mountain to meet with God, the people did not want to go. They just said, "You go, Moses, and come back and tell us what God said." They did not want a first-hand experience. So only Moses actually climbed the mountain and heard God speak.

Was Moses afraid? Of course he was... he was terrified! But he went anyhow, and met with God "face to face." The rest of them played it safe, but in so doing they missed a lot. Every time we play it safe, we miss something.

Yes, I have heard about all the dangers and the risks. I know that there are sharks in the ocean and bears in the woods and the rocks are sharp and the hills are steep. Yes, I understand that somewhere out there lurks a mosquito with West Nile virus. I know that there are spiders in the trees and snakes in the grass, and that if you go where you've never been before you might step in something.

Yes, I am familiar with dog hair in the carpet, wrinkled clothes, bee stings, and calamine lotion! And I remember mama warning me that I could "catch my death of cold!"

In the area of personal relationships, I know that friends can let you down, that people aren't always kind, and that if you fall in love you will probably get hurt. C. S. Lewis said it best in his book "The Four Loves:"

"There is no safe investment. To love at all is to be vulnerable. Love anything, and your heart will certainly be wrung and possibly be broken. If you want to make sure of keeping it

intact, you must give your heart to no one, not even to an animal. Wrap it carefully round with hobbies and little luxuries; avoid all entanglements; lock it up safe in the casket or coffin of your selfishness. But in that casket – safe, dark, motionless, airless – it will change. It will not be broken; it will become unbreakable, impenetrable, and irredeemable. The alternative to tragedy, or at least to the risk of tragedy, is damnation. The only place outside Heaven where you can be perfectly safe from all the dangers and perturbations of love is Hell."

So there is something worse than the potential risk of all of the dangerous things that we face in life. It is to spend your life removed from risk and discomfort, and thereby removed from reality. It is the unspeakable tragedy of wasting the precious moments of your life playing it safe, and as a consequence, losing the meaning of it all.

Earlier in this book, I quoted a great old song which goes: "Every time I hear a newborn baby cry, or touch a leaf, or see the sky, then I know why; I believe!"

I *do* believe, O Lord. Help me not to protect myself from your touch, your voice, and your heart. Amen.

35

Remembering Malcolm

"If I heard his voice today I would still recognize it. But unless he lived to be over a hundred, he has probably been gone a long time."

He was a nine-year-old child in the body of a forty-four-year-old man. Whether there were any social welfare programs for him or not, I don't know. We never thought about it.

It was the 1950s, and I had the first job of my life, earning an average of about three dollars a day selling Coca-Cola at Rickwood Field, home of the Birmingham Barons baseball team. Malcolm also worked there, as he had for fifteen years or more, starting, I am sure, years before I was ever born. He also made three dollars a day, walking up and down the steep aisles of Rickwood selling Cokes, peanuts, popcorn, and scorecards. The rest of us boys were probably eleven or twelve years of age. All of us were mentally ahead of Malcolm. "I'm forty-four!" he would shout at us. "Y'all need to respect me!"

It still pains my heart when I think of the times that we treated him with anything but respect. Of course we said it was "all in fun," but Malcolm was an easy mark. He would fall for anything. He believed anything that we told him. Many laughs were at his expense. Of course we never hurt him physically because, though he shuffled along with one foot dragging behind, he was quite strong. But we must have hurt him in other ways with our taunting, our "practical jokes," and our tricks.

From my understanding, Malcolm had been watched carefully by his loving mother until she died. But after that, he had been on his own, vulnerable to insensitive twelve-year-olds and God knows what else.

After working this job for a couple of years the rest of us went on to other things. Then, a few years later when I was in high school, I attended a Barons game. There was Malcolm, still selling Cokes. I bought one from him. He remembered me, though he never learned any of our names. He always just called me "Hey Bud."

"Malcolm" was the only name I ever knew him by. I can still remember his twisted face and his bad eyes, his slumped shoulders and his cracked voice.

If I heard his voice today I would still recognize it. But, of course, I'm sure I won't hear that voice again. Unless he lived to be over a hundred, he has probably been gone a long time.

Yet, after all these years I am still haunted by his memory. He was slow-witted, lame, unattractive... just shuffling along on a job made for twelve-year-olds because he could do nothing else.

But Malcolm always showed up and did his job. Living on just a few dollars because that was all he could earn, he proudly wore that little paper cap and out-hustled all of us to sell that extra Coke and make another two cents.

Looking back over more than fifty years, I now greatly respect Malcolm for his character and his indomitable spirit. I admire him for working so hard with what little ability he had. I didn't notice it then, but now I see that he was quite a guy. I'm not even sure that he knew it... but he was.

But mostly, I am glad that I grew up and found a better way to live than by taunting people that appear to be different.

I have no desire to be in any group that accepts only those who look and act and think as they do. I found that these giants of peer-pressure only make us phony and superficial. I found that none of us has the right to look down on others just because they don't have what we have, or they can't do what we do, or they don't know what we know.

Actually, when I said that I "found a better way to live," that's only a part of it. The more complete truth is that I have met and am trying to follow a man who really cares very much for each one of the "Malcolms" of the world... a man who welcomes and loves all of these people that others would never invite to their social gatherings.

This man doesn't care what you've done or where you've been... or what color you are, or how smart you are... or what your reputation is... or how much money you have. To him it makes no difference how nice your house, your car, or your clothing is. He is as willing and ready to welcome a scruffy beggar or a lonely stadium vendor as a senator, governor, president, or king.

Perhaps even more so... because broken, guilty, weak, wounded people are often much more ready to receive his grace than are the self-reliant, the self-important, even the religious.

In a most stumbling way, I am trying to follow a man who never met anybody he didn't love, and who never turned down even the most unworthy ones that wanted to come to Him.

I believe that one day in the past, probably several years ago, this same man put his arm around old Malcolm and then said something like this:

"Put down your tray of Cokes, my friend; today I'm taking you home!"

And Malcolm left Birmingham and went to a place where he will be able to see and talk and understand better than you or I ever could. His body, his mind, and his spirit will finally be whole.

I am hoping that God might even somehow let him know that, after all these years, you are reading and thinking about him, and that I am remembering him and writing about him, with the respect that he wanted and should have had from me back in the fifties.

But I was only eleven, maybe twelve. Undoubtedly, in some ways I still am.

And some bright day, Malcolm, I would like to sit down beside you and look out over home plate together, and talk about all of those games when we watched Dick Littlefield and Tommy O'Brian and Country Brown and Norm Zauchin and Bobo Newsome playing for the Barons. I would buy you a Coke, in a cup, with ice, just like we used to sell for ten cents at Rickwood.

(By the way, Rickwood Field still stands today, on 12th Street West in Birmingham — the oldest baseball stadium in the country!)

I remember it well, Malcolm. I can still hear your voice. I can still see your face.

36

Saying A Kind Word

"Before the day is over, you will meet that person and possibly not even know it."

Nearly all of us, no matter who we are, have a huge fear of inadequacy, that we will be perceived as losers, or that we won't fit in, and that we will be laughed at or humiliated or disapproved. Because of this, we grow up under a lot of pressure.

God, how we long to belong! How much we constantly hope that we will be wanted and loved! What lengths we go to in our hopes to impress people! It's reflected in the clothes we wear, the houses we live in, the cars we drive, and the places we have been.

We feel better about ourselves if we perform well, or if our kids are beautiful, or if our lawn is trimmed, or even if our team wins the championship.

Every child and every adult wants to be in a place where they are accepted for who they are. They hope to measure up, praying that they will do an adequate job in what they try to do. They long to be free from that nagging feeling that they are not good enough, and from that horrible fear of being rejected.

Some of us overcompensate by being loud or boisterous or outgoing, and I have sometimes done that too. But as I was growing up, I was plagued by an extreme bashful under-confidence, a strong inward sense of inadequacy.

I remember walking the long way home to avoid having to greet somebody whom I feared would criticize the way I said "Hello." I remember being totally infatuated with a girl, but being so petrified with shyness and fear that I couldn't dial her phone number.

It was a gradual process of growing that helped me to realize that everybody was *not* looking at me, but instead they shared the same fears that I had. While I worried what they thought about me, they were worried about what I thought of them. But of course I wasn't thinking of them at all... just as they weren't thinking of me.

I don't believe that we ever totally get over our self-conscious fears, but we find places and people in our lives where we can feel that we are really welcome and wanted just as we are. Like a warm fireplace on a cold winter night, it is so very good to find such places and such people!

Until the day comes when we really see things clearly as they are, and learn to value ourselves solely because we are loved by God without the need for other validation (and we are not there yet) we all will still struggle with this.

But, I am writing this for the *other* people.

Please be aware that there are so many others who need the warmth of our fire. Wherever we go, there will be people who desperately need what we can give if we will just open our eyes, take the time, and make the effort. It doesn't matter whether we have money or talents, we *can* take a moment to validate someone, just to acknowledge their presence, just to give them a smile, or better yet, an encouraging word.

My brother Danny related to me recently how a small compliment to an eighty-year-old lady made her countenance just glow! She had obviously taken a lot of time to be made up and attired to look her best, and the fact that Danny noticed (and said something!) just made her day! No doubt that when she went home and hung up that dress, she thought to herself, "I will wear this one again!" And perhaps she even thought she would definitely go back to the same hairdresser.

I am not really a great example of this myself, but I do believe that I am learning to be more sensitive to how others might feel as they come in contact with me. The kid bagging groceries, the cashier, the precious little children going to school, so scared that they won't fit in — they all could benefit from a little friendly acknowledgment. Particularly the ones who *don't* fit in, because for some reason they aren't among the "cool." These people are crying and they are dying... with increasing pain day by day... trying to live with the lack of at least a kind word from someone... anyone.

It reminds me of something another brother of mine (Joe) told me recently. He had gone to school with a boy that most people considered fat, and though my brother was not a close friend of his during school, at least he was nice to him and didn't call him names. Joe related to me that fifteen years later he happened to see him at a movie theater, and this young man was just so thrilled to see Joe, acting as if they had been long-lost close friends! He told my brother, "I can't believe it has been fifteen years since we were together!"

Then it occurred to my brother Joe that this precious person, this overweight but very decent guy, this man who was loved by God and undoubtedly had some very special qualities, had probably *never* had many other friends. There had not been much "together" in his life. Just treating him with a little bit of kindness had put Joe on an unfortunately short list.

Somewhere right now there is a little child, or a teenager, or a housewife, or a working man, or a senior citizen who is fighting back the tears that come from loneliness and rejection. Some of them aren't very popular or stylish or cool. They think that nobody understands and that nobody cares.

Before the day is over you will meet that person and possibly not even know it. Will you say a kind word to them? Can you give a sincere compliment? Is there something you can do to make their day, or maybe their life, better?

Somebody out there needs it so badly; they may still remember you in fifteen years.

37

Some Lessons from Mixed-Breed Dogs

"He has given us these wonderful creatures that never knew their daddy and forgot about their mama, but they wag their tails and think that we are the greatest thing since sliced bacon."

Every time I look at the back of my right hand and see that two-inch long scar, I think of Scottie. He was a bulldog-bird dog mix, the kind of dog that people give away if they can find anybody who wants one. But to a boy, his dog is the greatest thing in the world.

A loyal dog will adore its owner, who may have many shortcomings, but to the dog he is a god. The same respect is returned to the dog only by little boys.

We got Scottie when he was just a puppy, and I could not believe my dad when he said he was free. "*This* dog had to have cost hundreds of dollars, dad. Who would *give* away such a smart and beautiful and sweet puppy?" Of course, beauty is in the eye of the beholder, even with dogs.

From the time I was six, he was my most trusted friend, always wanting to go wherever I went, and I would have taken him to school with me if I could. Once I did, and they made me take him home. My teachers were so narrow-minded.

Anyway, here's the story of how I got the scar on my hand.

I was somewhere around thirteen, and puberty was making me think my folks were stupid and I knew more than they did. I talked back to my mother in a loud voice one night, and she told me to go outside until I could "straighten up." I slammed the door, and then for good measure I put my fist through the window glass, ripping a huge gash in my hand.

But I was too proud (or maybe too angry) to go back inside, so Scottie and I took off away from home. Wrapping my hand in newspapers, I walked eight miles through Birmingham, from Ensley on the west side to Woodlawn on the east side of the city. Of course Scottie was right there with me, never more than a few feet away. We walked through downtown, past the steel mills, through the neighborhoods to my grandmother's house. It took us four hours.

My grandmother gave me a hug, took me inside, bandaged my hand, and called my parents to let them know that I was okay and that I would be staying the night with her. Scottie, who had never been to her house, lay down on her front porch as I went inside. It was by now past midnight.

I thought that he would stay there on my grandmother's porch. But the next morning when I woke up, Scottie was gone. I called him and walked around the yard and through my grandmother's neighborhood, but Scottie could not be found. He had been my closest companion for seven years, and now I had lost him... all because of my own rebellion against my mother and my stubborn attitude which made me walk eight miles rather than turn around and apologize.

I prayed and I cried and repented. "Please, God, all I want is my little dog back! I will be better from now on, I promise!"

After a long search for my dog, we finally had to give up. Sometime around noon my grandmother drove me on a sad trip back to where I lived.

But upon arriving home, as we were coming up the steep steps in front, there was Scottie, waiting for me on the porch! He was so tired, but he was home! My mother said he got there just before we did, and he had collapsed from exhaustion, so weak that he had bumped his head as he lay down.

Looking down at this faithful little animal on my porch, I wondered how many miles Scottie had walked as he sniffed his way through the city of Birmingham for more than twelve hours. I thought about how many times he must have come close to being hit by a car as he sought to find the way home through the downtown traffic. I wondered what had driven him to keep going, and how he could find his way at all, with all the confusing noises and smells of the city. But I was so glad that he had made it, and was so grateful that he was back with me!

Lying down on the porch beside Scottie, I put my arm around him, amazed at the resilience and instincts of a common, mixed-breed, free dog.

Today, I am still amazed that the best things in life are indeed free. What we can earn or achieve or purchase is nothing compared to what God provides for us at no charge. It's called "grace," and it really is free. And it really is, as the hymn says, amazing!

And, just as a reminder of His faithfulness, He has given us these wonderful creatures that never knew their daddy and forgot about their mama, but they wag their tails and think we are the greatest thing since sliced bacon.

Looking back, I ask myself some questions about what really happened on that day that I broke the window and ran away with my dog to Grandma's house.

Did God really answer a boy's panicked prayer? Did almost losing my canine companion make me appreciate him more? Can humans learn from animals something about loyalty and determination? As I grew up, would I ever do anything that stupid again?

The answers are yes, yes, yes, and "Are you kidding?"

It was not the last scar that I got, nor the last mistake I made.

But sometimes when I really do mess something up and I have disappointed everybody and I know that my approval rating is zero... it is then that I know God has provided something very special... something that will make me feel like I am still okay, still wanted, and that, whatever I have done, I am still just a fantastically great guy.

This incredible gift... this faithful friend... is right over there, waiting behind the fence, wagging his tail.

[The following is just a parable from my own imagination, meant to show my gratitude for one small part of God's creation. It is not meant to be taken as literally true or theologically correct.]

God looked down from Heaven one day and saw how people were getting so many wrong ideas about what He was like.

He sadly listened to them as they spoke about an angry and un-reasonable God, one that was harsh and demanding and almost impossible to please. Being very dismayed, He wondered, "How can I show all these people that I just want to love them and receive them and forgive them? How can I show them that I have compassion on them and my love is not based on the requirement of good performance? How can I relate to them that my love is unconditional? How can I let them know that their lives are meant to be lived joyfully and gratefully, that life is a gift I have generously given to them just because I delight in who they are and what they mean to me?'

God thought for a while and then said, "I want to do something a little different from what anybody has ever seen! I think this will be fun, and it will illustrate to everybody my feelings for them. So I will make something that is very, very special to give to them."

With a twinkle of excitement in His eyes, God continued. "I will make one amazing animal that will come in many different sizes and shapes and colors. I will give each of them a unique personality. Some will be smart, and some will be kind of dumb. Some will be beautiful, and some will be ugly. Some will be more like a little wind-up toy, and others will be big and fierce looking. With a few exceptions, the bigger they are, the gentler they will be. But one thing will they all have in common: like me, they will love unconditionally. Like me, they will patiently wait for the one they love to just spend a few cherished moments with them. Whether the one they are waiting for is a pauper or a king or a criminal, they won't let it make any difference in their loyalty and love and affection. No matter how long they have to wait, they will always be so eager and happy to see the ones they love. To them, they will happily greet every meeting as if it has been a long long time since they have been together. And, as more than just a coincidence, I will give them a name that is the same as mine, only backward!"

So God gave us these amazingly faithful creatures, and even put a tail on the rear end, and not just a tail like other creatures have, but one that even wags back and forth, just for something extra to show their pleasure at our presence! And all of Heaven rejoiced that God had come up with such a novel way to show to all people His love and friendship and joy!

Even from my childhood, how many times have I felt that I didn't have a friend in the world, but... my dog was there.

How many times have I felt like I was a fool and a failure? Maybe I struck out with the bases loaded. Maybe I failed the big test. Maybe the current "love of my life" took off with somebody else. Maybe I just messed up everything with everybody in my life.

But... my dog was there.

Even today, when I feel misunderstood or mistreated, I find comfort in these sweet, loving creatures. How anyone could ever abuse one is beyond my understanding.

And when as a husband I do or say something stupid or insensitive and I am sent to the doghouse... well, my dog will just wag his tail and happily move over to make room for me.

President Harry Truman said, "If you want to have a friend in Washington, get a dog!" The same is true in many other places too.

To me, this article will be worthwhile if just one person will go to a local animal shelter and rescue his or her potential best friend who anxiously waits in a cage on death row.

So... here's to Jip, the part-chow; and to Butch, who got hit by a car while running toward me after school; and Scottie, the bulldog-bird dog mix who spent nine years as my best friend; and Morgan, the greatest squirrel-hunting Boston Terrier who ever lived; and Princess and Sugar and Leonard Parker and Maggie and Ben; and eight-pound Muffin, who rules inside our house; and sweet old useless Hunter, and destructive little Beecher, who places land mines throughout our back yard; and my grand-dog Henry, the Yorkie who thinks he's a Labrador; and poor old Lucky, and so many others who looked to me with eyes of trust and were so delighted to spend some time with me even if nobody else wanted to.

I hope that I was as good a friend to you as you were to me. Thank you for being in my life.

One evening I sat down in the back yard to pray, and my dog sat beside me, looking up at me and wagging his tail. I said, "Dear Lord, help me to want to be with you as much as this dog wants to be with me."

And God said, "That will never happen, but the point is that I want to be with *you* as much as the dog does!"

Thank you, God... for four-legged grace.

38

The 1948 Plymouth

*"Then the next day, Dad decided to wash his car, and
I will never forget what happened next."*

Having only a tenth-grade education and having been
raised in poverty, my father never had a driver's license or a car
until I was about ten years old. Occasionally, my mother would
borrow my grandmother's car and drive it. But my father, who
always had a great work ethic, would ride the bus or the street-
car to his job every day.

Finally he got a license and saved up enough money to
buy a used car — our family's first automobile! We were all so
proud of it when he drove it home. It was a powder-blue 1948
Plymouth sedan. My dad had really worked hard to be able to
make this purchase.

Unfortunately, it only took a few hours before he realized
that he had been "ripped off."

Driving down the road with all of us, the car just quit running. Somehow he got it running again, but soon it quit the second time. Somehow we got it going and made it back home.

Then the next day, Dad decided to wash his car... and I will never forget what happened next.

When he started washing the car it was blue, but by the time he had finished washing it, it was yellow! Actually, the blue had mixed with the yellow in some places, making it green in those places. I looked at this old Plymouth as my father tried to hold back the tears. Part of it was still blue. Part of it was green. But most of it was yellow. Dad had bought a used-up taxi cab. The old car was worn out, probably with over 200,000 miles, and back in 1948 they didn't build cars to last that long.

So, for a long time, it was back to riding the bus to work. Then, one day, he took me with him and he bought a decent 1951 Ford, which he drove for many years.

I was thinking about this recently, and I could still see my father with that hose and bucket of water, washing that car as the yellow came through. Here's something that I thought of:

We all need to be cleansed — from our sins, our many faults, our stubbornness and our pride, but when we do experience cleansing, our "true colors" come out, and we see that we were not at all what we pretended to be. Underneath our carefully sprayed-on shiny exterior is something that is not so attractive. There are many wounds and scratches, many faded and worn fabrics, many evidences that we have had some hard times and put in some rough miles going down some bumpy roads. We've had collisions with other "cars." We've neglected the necessary "maintenance." We've tried to run on bad "gasoline." We've allowed ourselves to become rusty and dirty. We've taken many wrong turns and gone too fast down the wrong "highways!"

(You could probably add a few other metaphors here!)

But we need to face it and deal with it. As soon as we do, it can be the beginning of a new chapter in our Carfax history!

My father did not keep the old Plymouth, and it probably rusted away in a junk yard a long time ago. What had once been a shiny new sedan finally, mercifully, is off the road forever.

But, to continue this analogy, here is some really good news! There are some amazingly talented and patient people (bless their hearts!) who will take an old car, fix everything about it, and restore it to its original condition or even better! It is a long and expensive process, but these guys who restore old cars are able to see the value and potential of the automobile... enough to want to put a lot of time and work and money and love into it. They envision the finished product and gladly do what is necessary.

Of course, my point is that God looks at *us* that way! As the saying goes, "Beauty is in the eyes of the beholder." And when the Great Restorer sees us as potentially beautiful, well... you and I are no longer just "clunkers," we are "classics!"

Sometimes I see myself as just an old worn-out taxicab. But the fact is that I am a classic that is still being restored!

I am not very proud of myself when the blue washes off, and the old taxi yellow color first appears.

But when the restoration is finally completed... Wow! I will really shine!

39

The Chair in My Yard

"The point is that I am there, alone, but not alone, and something seems to let me know that everything is okay and in good hands."

In my back yard, sitting about fifty feet out from my back door, is an old plastic chair. Sometimes the dog or the wind turns it over, and many times the old chair is neglected and stays turned over for a while.

But the chair is there for a unique purpose. It's impossible for me to describe how or why it works the way it does, but it is meaningful enough in my life that I wanted to share it with you.

On occasion (not regularly enough, probably) I walk out to that chair and just quietly sit there. Please understand that I am not there to be talking things over with myself, or even with God. It is different from praying, and I am not there to think about things. I am only there to do one thing... to listen.

Sometimes it takes a while to clear the thoughts from my mind. When I find myself focusing on a particular problem or subject, I have to try to get beyond that, so that there is no concern for the past or the future, but only an awareness of the present moment and my present surroundings. If I am thinking or talking or worrying or figuring things out, I am not there yet. My purpose for being there is different. It is not *wrong* to do any of these things, but that is not the purpose of the chair.

Then, if it works right, finally, I will begin to notice the brightness of the day, or the darkness of the night, or the sound of a lone cricket, or the song of a bird. I become conscious of my breathing, and I feel the slightest gentle breeze upon my face. When that happens, I try to continue that way for as many minutes as I can. Sometimes it is for five minutes, and sometimes it is thirty minutes or more. But everything else needs to stop so that whatever time I am there is not clouded or crowded by anything else.

Here is the strange part. For the life of me I don't know why it is or how it works, but it does! After these times in the chair, things seem to come together better in my life. As far as I know it doesn't make me any smarter or wiser, and sometimes I feel that it has been a total waste of time. Sometimes I feel like I have been sitting at a blank wall of nothingness. But, for some reason, life seems better after an episode in the chair. I am more grateful for what I have. Problems don't upset me as much. I begin to see myself as a small part of something big instead of a big part of something small. The shadow of gloom that haunts so many of us seems to disappear. Anger and regret and fear and so much wasted mental energy begin to appear as they really are, which is that they are silly and insignificant and not deserving of our attention.

Some people call this "meditation." Some call it "centering prayer." Some would say that those are not the same, and I am doing it all wrong. And, of course, some would say that I am just weird. It could be a mixture of all of these; I don't know.

But, in the most humble way that I can, I want to recommend that you try it.

Sometimes it has been difficult for me to enter into this, because I am the kind of person who wants to understand what is going on. I think that I have a need to have things figured out. To be honest, I am a reformed and repentant control freak from way back!

But, sitting in that chair, I must relinquish my illusions of control and give up my demands for all the answers on a rational level. Sitting in that chair, I know that being a control freak is self-deception, and that I can't control anything. And that is good, not bad.

If you ever fly in a plane, and you are not the pilot, it is the same idea. Holding on to the seats and biting your fingernails will not affect how the plane flies, or how it lands. You got on the plane, now you are in someone else's hands. This whole machine with everything in it has somehow left the ground. Now, you can either enjoy the trip or you can cringe and sweat and throw up. Either way, you can't get off now, and wherever the plane goes is where you will go.

Sitting in that chair... regardless of how the circumstances of my life are going... whether I have been getting it right or doing it wrong... all is well!

Let me go even further: whether my life has recently been obediently faithful or full of sin... it doesn't change anything. The point is that I am there, alone but not alone, and something or someone else seems to let me know that everything is okay and in good hands.

I may feel very uncomfortable about it if my life has not been in line with what it should be. But the chair is not for perfect people. It is for anybody who wants to be there.

Nobody can *use* that chair to get something done for himself. You can't use it to get what you want, even if what you want is wisdom or knowledge or "spiritual experience." It's just a place and a time to become open. That's all.

Without a doubt, the One who made the sun and the stars and the earth and all of us who live here is so much bigger than my understanding of theology or religion. None of us will ever fully see the Holy One in all of His majesty and glory. We just couldn't take it if we did.

But could it be possible (though He fills the universe and is transcendent and separate from His creation) that He is also closer than I dare to think? Could it be that His voice can be heard in the sound of a little cricket? Perhaps, could His presence be felt even in a slight gentle breeze?

If you want to find out more... I have some bad news and some good news:

The bad news is that you may investigate this, and you will find a hundred different opinions on what this is all about and why it works or seems to work for people, and you will probably never understand it.

But here is the good news:

Your chair is waiting.

40

The Monster Movie

"Just an hour before, I had been proud and self-assured. Now I was just a frightened, lost little boy. I was in a living nightmare."

I had seen the previews of a monster movie entitled "Creature from the Black Lagoon." Though I was only eleven years old, I had made up my mind that as soon as it hit the screen, I just had to see it! Normally, if we went to a movie, it would be on a Saturday when school was out, and we would usually go to a neighborhood theater which showed double-features of movies that had been out for a while. Only the downtown theaters showed first-run features, and the tickets were more expensive.

But, when "Creature from the Black Lagoon" came out, I couldn't wait! I had saved up forty cents, which was enough money to ride the bus to the Strand Theater in downtown Birmingham and still have enough for a ticket to the movie. So when the movie first arrived, on the first day, I walked alone from my house to the bus stop and paid the bus fare to go downtown.

Did I ask my parents if I could go? Did I tell them where I was going? I honestly don't remember if I did or not. I do remember being so happy just to feel like I was on my own, just like a grown-up... buying my own ticket... making my own decisions... watching what I wanted to watch, when I wanted to watch it, by golly!

The thrill of my independence, the excitement of the movie, even the fact that I was brave enough to dare to watch such a scary motion picture — all of it was exhilarating to me. "Finally, I am not a little kid any more!"

I watched "The Creature from the Black Lagoon" not just once but three times that day in the movie theater. What a great time I had... nobody to tell me what to do, nobody to tell me how to act. I did exactly as I pleased, and it was great! Besides, once you pay to get in you can stay as long as you want, so I was getting my money's worth.

All of these years later, I can still remember the sudden and drastic change that sent shock waves through me as I left the Strand after the third screening of the "Creature." Walking outside, I saw that it was dark. I was hungry, I was tired... and I was lost.

I didn't know where the bus stop was, and I didn't know which bus to take or even which direction to go. I couldn't remember if I lived on the east side of town, or maybe the west side, or was it north? I didn't know if I lived five miles away, or ten, or more. When you're a little boy, the city is so big, and you don't know how far a mile is anyway! In the ecstasy of my adventurous trip to town, I had never thought that later it might be nice to know how to go home!

Then I remembered something even worse: even if I had known which bus to take, I had no money for a ticket. Fifteen cents for the bus to go downtown and twenty-five cents for the movie, and my forty-cent budget was depleted. I had never even thought about the return trip!

Frantically and hopefully, I began to walk through the downtown streets of Birmingham, looking to try to find some familiar place that might give me an idea of which way to walk home. In desperation and confusion, I circled around several times, coming back to the same spots.

Just an hour before, I had been proud and self-assured. Now I was a just a frightened, lost little boy. A sense of absolute panic gripped me. My throat tightened, and my knees buckled. I was in a living nightmare. On top of that, my mind had been so filled with the "Creature" movie that I started imagining that the creature had left the theater with me and was following me!

I had been holding back the tears for over an hour, but they finally burst through and flooded my face. I cried as if my heart had been broken. I thought of mom, and dad, and home. I just stood on a downtown street corner and wept bitterly.

Fortunately, it wasn't long before a kind couple noticed my tears and got me to blubber out my phone number. They put a nickel in a pay phone and called my parents, who were, as we say in the South, "worried sick." Soon I was on the way home, though I can't remember how I got there. When I arrived it was dark and very late, but the light was still on and the door was open. I had reached the house safely, and all was well!

Despite the incredibly stupid thing that I had done, nobody punished me or lectured me about it. Dad said that I had suffered enough and that I had learned my lesson. He also said that he was just so glad to see me that he couldn't even think of giving me a whipping.

Please notice my last sentence again, if you will. It tells a remarkable truth that I don't want anybody to miss. It is a story of pure grace, of unconditional love. My father said that he was just so happy to see me that punishing me never even crossed his mind!

Many years ago Jesus illustrated this amazing concept of grace by means of a simple story which he told to some religious leaders because they were "too good" to welcome common sinners. It was about a prodigal son who returned home after a long journey that had begun in defiance and rebellion. Though the son had sinned foolishly and frivolously, his father was just so overjoyed to see him that he didn't even think about punishing him. The father just simply *ran* to him, kissed him, hugged him, gave him gifts, and called for a steak dinner, music, and a celebration!

The message of the story is clear: this is the way God feels toward his children when we go astray. With open arms, He longs for us to come home.

Even the opening chapters of Scripture reveal to us a God who walked into the garden at dusk, looking for his disobedient children and calling, "Where are you?"

When I was watching the "Creature" movie for the third time, it never occurred to me that back home there was a kind father and mother, as well as my younger brothers, who were waiting and worrying and praying and hoping for my safe return. They didn't even have a car back then. But they were there, waiting not with anger, but with a desire to love and accept and welcome me home.

If you have gone astray, whether carelessly or deliberately (and all of us have,) you are missed... and you are still wanted... and you are so very welcome to come back home!

No matter where you are, or what you've done, or where you've been, or how long you've been gone, please know this: the door is still open, and the light is still on. There is no lecture awaiting, no punishment in store, and no scathing rebuke about how wrong you were. Instead, there are tears and hugs and kisses, music and dancing and laughter, and great joy!

The undeserved and seemingly unreasonable grace of God is best demonstrated by the laughter and music coming from a welcome-home party given in honor of a wretched wayward son who has limped back home to the father's house.

When you do come home, all of the other people there at the party will understand... because they too have gone too far, sunk too low, and stayed away too long. But our Father says that it just doesn't matter any more, now that you're home! And deep down inside you will wonder why you waited so long to join the party.

In fact, when you start to hear the music playing, you will remember that you've heard it before, a long time ago... even when you were a child.

41

The Pitcher Who Sang

"On that night, Johnny Carson was speechless. The blood had drained from his face, leaving it a ghostly white."

It was October 21, 1988. The World Series had just ended with a five-game victory for the Los Angeles Dodgers. The star of that series, as well as the star for the entire season, was a slightly built, soft-spoken young pitcher named Orel Hershiser.

Orel Hershiser may never be chosen for the Hall of Fame because the Hall of Fame takes into consideration the entire career of a player, and Hershiser did not have a great and long career. But in 1988 there was nobody like him. He led the league with 23 wins, led the league with 267 innings pitched, and in complete games pitched with fifteen. Most remarkable of all, he set a record that still stands today: pitching 59 consecutive scoreless innings!

Think of that: this man faced more than two hundred major league batters in a row, and not once did a runner cross the plate. As a result, Hershiser won every major-league award for that year, including the Cy Young award, National League MVP, and World Series MVP.

In the last game of the World Series, which, of course, I watched on television, Hershiser finally did allow a couple of runs. Other runners were on base. The partisan Oakland crowd was cheering for their team and booing Hershiser. Screaming and taunting him, they were pulling for their guys to get another hit and drive the runners in and win the game against Hershiser. In the midst of all of that noise, he walked off to the back side of the pitcher's mound and took just a minute to be by himself under all that pressure. Amazed, the TV announcer said, "I think he is singing!"

Orel Hershiser stepped back to the mound and eventually got the batter out and won the game and the series for his team. As a lifelong baseball fan, I have never seen such a performance as this man gave for the year 1988.

For those of us who remember that time, you know that late night television was dominated by one man for nearly thirty years, the one-of-a-kind host of the Tonight Show, Johnny Carson. Carson's staff immediately arranged to get Orel Hershiser as a special guest, and they landed him to be on the show on October 21.

I watched it that night, not knowing that it would be (for me) the most unforgettable Tonight Show I would ever watch.

The crowd cheered when Orel Hershiser was introduced that night, and after a few pleasantries and a few funny lines from Carson, the conversation settled down and got serious.

From his famous Tonight Show desk, Johnny Carson

spoke. "Orel, when the pressure was on you in that last game, and the crowd was screaming for you to lose the game, someone said that you stepped back and sang a song. Is that right?'

"Yes sir," Hershiser said softly.

Johnny Carson then asked him if he would sing it for the audience. The audience applauded, encouraging him to sing it for them.

"Well, I'm really not much of a singer," Hershiser said. But Johnny insisted, and the audience began to chant, "Sing it! Sing it! Sing it!"

What happened next I shall never forget.

Orel Hershiser took a deep breath as Carson and the audience got quiet. Hershiser began to sing with a soft, sincere and trembling voice, the old tune that we always called "The Doxology:"

Praise God from whom all blessings flow

Praise Him all creatures here below

Praise Him above ye heavenly hosts

Praise Father, Son, and Holy Ghost.

Now, I must confess that I very often watched the Tonight Show, and Johnny Carson always had a funny comeback for any situation. But on that night, friends, Johnny Carson was speechless. The blood had drained from his face, leaving it a ghostly white. Throughout the NBC audience you could have heard a pin drop. Everything stood silent and still. Staring at the television, I felt a Presence in the room... and I believe that people all over the country also felt it.

And in that Hollywood studio, which was certainly not designed to be a church or a "house of worship," the Spirit of the Lord showed up!

It was not the loud thundering of a trained preacher, nor the great efforts of a worldwide Christian organization. It was the just the soft voice and humble spirit of a baseball player who sang praises to God in the right place at the right time. And it flabbergasted a great entertainer and his entire audience.

Sometimes it doesn't take much... just faithfulness to let our light shine in the right place at the right time.

As another song says, "Little is much — when God is in it."

42

The Truth About Christmas

*"It was not a silent night; all was not calm; all was
not bright. It wasn't 'beginning to look a lot like
Christmas.' There was no winter wonderland, not one
jingle bell, and no drummer boy."*

As we approach the most celebrated holiday in the world,
there is one thing of which we can all be certain. None of us
can ignore Christmas, and none of us can escape it. It's in every
song and event and circumstance. Christmas is in the traffic, in
the malls, in the churches, and on the streets. It's in the noise of
the city and in the quietness of the countryside. It's in the
scurry of the shoppers and in the stillness of the cold winter air.

I must confess that many times I have approached the
Christmas season with the attitude of Scrooge. I've found myself wishing for all of it to just be over with for another year. To
me, shopping is a major ordeal, and I feel that I can never pick
the right gift for anybody on my list. And I know my list is

flawed, and I probably forgot somebody.

The ideal Christmas was always a dream that was never realized. Having been brought up in a culture where the Currier and Ives scenes, the Norman Rockwell paintings, and the Bing Crosby and Bob Hope Christmas specials extolled an image of the perfect holiday, I was set up for disappointment every year. I never saw a "white Christmas." The treetops didn't glisten, and the children didn't hear sleigh bells in the snow. Never once has our whole extended family sat on the hearth in matching outfits, smiling with perfect teeth and singing in perfect harmony.

What I do remember are misshapen Christmas trees with lights that didn't work, songs that were a little off-key, and gifts that were the wrong size. Worse than that, I remember a Christmas that was ruined by alcohol abuse, and another one when a family member became angry and cussed everybody out. On one Christmas day some good friends decided to get a divorce. And there was the Christmas Eve when our car engine blew up on the way to Grandma's house. Not to mention the times when somebody got sick, and the Christmases when we just couldn't get everybody together.

I have come to believe that my experiences are not unique. I suspect that many of the Christmases in your life have been similar to mine — grand expectations thwarted by stark disappointment, even disillusion. Sadly, there are more suicides during the Christmas season than at any other time of year.

Yet, most of us do keep trying, don't we? Though the perfect Christmas doesn't happen, a lot of us have finally become willing to settle for a "pretty good" one. Maybe this year we will get it mostly right, and most of us can come, and we will all mostly get along. Maybe this time the gifts will fit, the lights will shine, nobody will get mad, and the angels will sing.

Maybe...

The thought occurs to me that on that first Christmas in Bethlehem there was not an ideal atmosphere. Though I love the song, it was not a silent night; all was not calm; all was not bright. It wasn't "beginning to look a lot like Christmas," there was no winter wonderland, not one jingle bell, and no drummer boy. The manger smelled bad. The stable was dark and crowded. The mooing of cattle, the braying of donkeys, and the barking of dogs kind of messed up the carol singing. Instead of reindeer, there were likely rats and snakes slithering on the muddy floor. Even the wise men showed up two years late.

Neither Mary nor her baby had halos over their heads. People rushing by did not know nor care what had happened. This baby came into a dark world that was in "as-is" condition. There was nothing "Christmassy" about it. Then, as now, the ideal Christmas was only a fantasy.

Putting all romanticism and fantasy aside, however, something very real did happen in Bethlehem that night. All of life and all of history was changed forever as a result of the simple, obscure birth of a little baby who was conceived by an unmarried woman, born in a makeshift delivery room by the side of the road, and raised in a simple and poor Jewish home. Whoever or whatever you may believe him to be, his enormous impact on the entire world continues today, and cannot be denied.

So, to celebrate this mysterious event, it is only fitting that we have come up with a few hundred things! So let's waste no more time, and let the celebration begin! Let's have parties, and pageants, and presents for everybody! Bring on the jolly man with the red suit and the elves and the red-nosed reindeer! Get the holly and the mistletoe, the eggnog and the cookies! Wrap everything in ribbons and bows, and decorate it all with bright colored lights! Close the schools and the shops, get family and friends together from far and near! Decorate a tree, decorate your house and your lawn and your dogs and your cats; even decorate your kids and yourselves, and sing songs about it all! Laugh and dance and dream once again that *you* are a child, because all things have been made new again!

Fantasy? Yes, but it is a fantasy created in honor of, and in celebration of, an awesome reality! And even if it never comes together just right, that's okay. How can we *not* celebrate?

Merry Christmas to all!

43

Three Who Did Not Fall

"These men are about to pass from our midst, after all of these years. Soon we will look back and remember how they shined so brightly for so long."

It was late at night and I couldn't sleep. I surfed through the TV channels and landed on C-Span. The program I saw has occupied my thoughts for several days since then. It was the rebroadcast of the dedication of the new Billy Graham Library in North Carolina.

The ceremony had taken place under a huge tent on a warm sunny day. Among the guests were former presidents Carter, Bush, and Clinton, plus about a hundred senators, congressmen and governors, as well as many ministers and business leaders. About a thousand invited guests were there, as were all of the veteran members of the Billy Graham team.

Each of the former presidents spoke of the impact of Billy Graham on their lives and upon this country and on the world.

Many of the dignitaries spoke to give honor to the life of this man and his ministry. All of that was as expected.

But it seemed to me that there was a noticeable change in the atmosphere when (finally) three old white-haired men stood up. All three needed canes to help them walk. These three men had traveled together as an evangelistic team for sixty years. At the time of this ceremony, Cliff Barrows was eighty-four. Billy Graham was eighty-eight. George Beverly Shea was ninety-eight.

[Note: at the time of this book going to press, these men were all still with us, and George Beverly Shea has now turned 102!]

My mind suddenly traveled back in time to the huge football stadium called Legion Field in Birmingham, when this team first came to town during a period of intense racial strife. City officials were worried, and the KKK was tearing down the Billy Graham signs and threatening violence. Somebody had roped off sections marked "white only" and "colored." Billy Graham had personally walked into the stands and pulled down the ropes! Inside the stadium, love and peacefulness prevailed!

I remembered how he had preached with those blazing blue eyes, pure and strong and bold. I remembered the awesome choir led by Cliff Barrows, who always knew when and how to say the right thing in front of a crowd. I remembered the resonant voice of George Beverly Shea singing. His song made such an impact on me that I memorized these words:

Could we with ink the oceans fill, and were the skies of parchment made.

Were every stalk on earth a quill, and every man a scribe by trade

To write the love of God above would drain the oceans dry

Nor could the scroll contain the whole, though stretched from sky to sky.

Oh love of God, how rich and pure, how measureless and strong!

It shall forevermore endure the saints and angels' song.

Again I looked at the TV screen as these three elderly men hobbled to the podium.

Cliff Barrows was still eloquent, but his voice trembled when he spoke.

Billy Graham had difficulty walking, his hands shook, and his voice was very weak. Everybody laughed when he said it felt to him like he was attending his own funeral. You could tell that he meant it when he said that his impression of the library was that there was "too much Billy Graham." He did not want to take any glory, which he said "should only go to Christ."

George Beverly Shea had to be helped as he tried to stand, but that great singing voice was still incredibly strong! How moving it was to hear him once again sing "How Great Thou Art!"

I listened very attentively to what these three men had to say, and the way they said it. They were so different from the dignitaries and the politicians present. There was an aura of peacefulness and a deep humility. They were comfortable as they sang and talked about God. To them, God was not a high and unapproachable deity, but instead seemed to be their closest friend.

I was alone in my dark living room, and when it was over I turned the TV off. It was now past midnight, but I was wide awake and filled with awe as I thought of how these three men had committed their whole lives to this one ministry.

If you and I someday live into our eighties and beyond, I think that most of us will probably have more regrets than do these three men. But we can make our lives count for something.

The message of God's grace teaches us that it is never too late, that no one is so bad that he can't be forgiven, yet no one is so good that they don't need to be. Even our failures, if we are willing, can be used as an encouragement and a ministry to others who fail.

None of these men would ever deny that they, too, are sinners. They would, in fact, be quick to tell you that they are. But here is an amazing fact:

Since they first started traveling together back in the 1940s, none of these men has ever become driven by ego, nor allowed his ministry to become divisive over politics or religious denominations.

None of them has ever had an extramarital affair with another woman or man.

You never heard about any of them living a lavish lifestyle, or being involved with questionable activities, or greedy with money.

None of them has cheated on his taxes or been caught in the wrong place doing the wrong thing.

None of them ever has been heard to make an unkind or off-color remark. Not even once.

Looking at these men with their stumbling steps, their wrinkled skin, their various ailments and aches and pains, it serves as a reminder that we all are slowly dying. But I also am filled with wonder at these sweet, gentle, beautiful men, totally consumed in doing one great work together for their entire lives!

For sixty years they left the warmth of their homes to go around the world. In obedience to what they believed was a divine call, they put every other dream aside. Faithfully through the late forties and through the fifties, the sixties, the seventies, the eighties, the nineties, and even into this century, they traveled and prayed and sang and served and preached.

Sometimes just before the sermon by Mr. Graham, George Beverly Shea would sing these words:

"It took a miracle to put the stars in place. It took a miracle to hang the world in space, but when he saved my soul, cleansed and made me whole, it took a miracle of love and grace."

These men never called their meetings "miracle crusades." Their entire lives were a miracle!

These men are about to pass from our midst, after all of these years. They await their reward on the other side. Soon we will look back and remember how they shined so brightly for so long.

The methods and styles changed over the years, but the message was always the same. A message that they felt was worth all of their efforts and more.

It was the story of a cross... and an empty tomb... and of a love that could not be fully told... even if the oceans were ink, and the skies were parchment.

44

What About "The World?"

If you meet a person who has an alcohol problem or is homeless or is in prison or struggles with addictive behavior, listen to the cry of their heart, their desire to be free."

After I had a conversion experience at the age of nineteen, I was trying so hard to be a good and godly person. It was a noble adventure and full of joy. I had found a new life, and I was deeply immersed in it. Even today I can still remember the incredible peace and happiness that I felt. My entire existence was like a dream come true, and God allowed me to live in that dream for more than two years. During that time nothing else mattered to me because I was enraptured by this experience.

The only down side of this was that during that time I was taught that this world is an evil place, that I should separate myself from it and not let it influence me in any way. "Don't listen to their music, don't go to any movies, don't let down your guard around the people of the world, lest ye get caught up in their ways."

I was probably one of the only people my age anywhere that hardly knew the difference between the Beatles and the Rolling Stones, and I couldn't have cared less. They were all "evil." I was taught that "worldliness" was a bad thing. I am aware that there are still millions of people being taught to be suspicious of the world outside if they don't totally agree with it and control it.

Gradually, and gratefully, I have come to believe differently concerning the world. I will admit that this is not very well organized, but these are just some of the things that at one time I was afraid to even think, but now I am not afraid to say. So here goes:

All truth is God's truth, wherever it may be found. If God can speak through a donkey, as has happened at least once, He can and often does speak great spiritual truth through a person who doesn't have his or her life together.

All people are created in the divine image, and though we are flawed and sinful, we still are the objects of His love. God always has delighted in bypassing the ones who would seem to be the most qualified, and speaking to and through the most unworthy.

So if you meet a person who has an alcohol problem, or is homeless, or is in prison, or struggles with addictive behavior — listen to the cry of their heart, their desire to be free. You will likely learn something you will never hear from the typical pulpit. You will learn non-judgmental compassion. You will see humility and authenticity. In their faces you will see the face of Christ.

There is a line in the old hymn "Am I a Soldier of the

Cross," that asks a rhetorical question "Is this vile world a friend to grace, to help me on to God?"

Well, friends, I know the answer is supposed to be no, but it *can* be yes!

I have come to believe that the message and ministry of Christ is not at all about staying away from the world until someday when we will be called out of it. We are to be bringing the kingdom of God into the place where we are, making it a better place to live, helping the sick and hungry and suffering, in this life, at this time, in this world!

And we certainly aren't following a savior who was reluctant to be around sinners! How sad that we have diluted this great gospel of the kingdom into "Just be saved and ready to go to heaven when you die." It is so very much more than that.

There is grace all around us, if we will just look for it. Take for example, dogs. I am a huge dog-lover. If my wife would let me, I would have twenty of them. I believe that it is no accident that dog is God spelled backward. When you are really down, nothing is more comforting than a sweet old dog who wags his tail and just wants to be with you. They give us their all in return for scraps. In it all, we see a creature that reflects the unconditional love and faithfulness of the one who made both the man and the dog.

[I know... I got in to this same thing in another chapter in this book. Thanks for not mentioning it!]

Once I wrote that if a man wanted to find out who is his most loyal friend in the world, he could try this experiment: take your wife and your dog, and lock them in the trunk of your car. Come back an hour later, and see which one is glad to see you!

I got a critical letter for writing what I had written, saying it was horrible and not the least bit funny. Guess who wrote it? Certainly not a dog!

Sometimes a little messenger of grace comes right to our doorstep, totally by surprise.

A few months ago my wife put up a decorative bird house right beside our back door... but a little wren didn't know that it was just a decoration and has now moved in and nested. Soon there will be a complete new feathered family on our porch!

The bird house hangs just five feet off the ground, but I look at it like the wren trusted us that we would not hurt or bother her or her new babies. And she was right. There is not enough money in the world to make me harm those little birds!

It appears that a little creature who hardly weighs an ounce has helped me to find some grace even in my own heart.

If you watch the news channels on television or listen to talk radio, you can get the impression that the world is full of crooks and murderers... that everywhere there are protests and arguments and fights, bombings and shootings and violence. I know that these things happen, and we should take them seriously, be careful, and work to try to stop it. I know that.

But if you turn off the TV and go to the park, or to the beach, or to a yard sale or a concert or a coffee shop, you will find that most of this world is full of beauty and honor and friendly peace-loving people.

Yes, you can say this world is evil, and separate yourself and hide from it so that you will not be contaminated.

But the greatest teacher who ever lived said that most of our problems come not from the outside, but from the inside.

"No matter where you go, there you are!"

I close with these words from a Louie Armstrong song:

I see trees of green, red roses too; I see them bloom for me and for you

And I think to myself what a wonderful world.

I see skies of blue and clouds of white; the bright blessed day, the dark sacred night

And I think to myself what a wonderful world.

The colors of the rainbow so pretty in the sky are also on the faces of people going by.

I see friends shaking hands saying how do you do. They're really saying I love you.

I hear babies crying, I watch them grow; they'll learn much more than I'll never know,

And I think to myself what a wonderful world.

Yes I think to myself what a wonderful world.

Oh yeah!

45

When Love Blows Us Away

"He couldn't continue to betray such trust and respect. Looking in the mirror, he vowed to become the kind of man that his wife believed him to be."

My heart was deeply touched by an e-mail I received which purportedly was telling a true story, a story about a little boy whose older sister had a rare and fatal blood disease. The little boy had developed in his own blood the antibodies that gave him immunity, but unfortunately his older sister had not. The doctors explained to him that if he did not give his blood to his sister, she would die.

Her little brother sat quietly for several minutes. He thought long and hard before finally agreeing to the blood transfusion. "I'm ready," he told the doctors. "You can start today."

Apparently someone had not fully explained everything to the little boy, because just as they started the transfusion, he asked another question. Looking up at the nurse with some sadness in his eyes, the question came from his lips: "Will I start to die right now?"

I have heard people talk spiritual talk and use a lot of religious language, and, frankly, as Shania says, "That don't impress me much!" Overly religious, "churchy" sermons usually bore me. However, when I come face to face with real, unpretentious, self-sacrificing *love* such as this little boy had, I must stop and take a breath and wipe away a tear. I know that I have, for just a moment, encountered something that is beyond normal human living — something that is divine.

A doctor named Richard Selzer writes of a surgery he performed to remove a tumor from the face of a young lady. In the surgery it was necessary that he clip a nerve, leaving her mouth grotesquely twisted. In his book he describes the scene in the hospital room.

The lady's husband is standing to the side. She asks the doctor, "Will my mouth always be like this?" The doctor replies, "Yes, because the nerve had to be cut." The doctor then stands amazed as her husband smiles at her and says, "I like it... it's kind of cute."

Consider Selzer's next words:

"All at once I know who he is. I understand and I lower my gaze. One is not bold in an encounter with a god. Unmindful, he bends over to kiss her crooked mouth, and I am so close that I can see how he twists his own lips to accommodate to hers, to show her that their kiss still works."

After so many people with the attitude of "I love her because she looks so appealing to me," or "I love him because he just makes me feel so happy," I am thrilled and blessed to hear about somebody who understands that love really is just the opposite of this kind of self-centeredness.

I believe that in spite of how jaded we may become, no matter how many phonies we may meet along the way, and regardless of how much disappointment and disillusionment we may experience, we are still "blown away" when we encounter this kind of love.

Usually, when we say "love" we may mean anything from lust to pleasure to mild affection. I "love" good music, a really funny joke, old cars, the sunrise, Cajun food, great books, sweet, faithful dogs, and ice cream.

The ancient Greeks had different words for various kinds of love. One meant a fondness for someone. Another meant a sense of belonging. Another meant sexual attraction. But the most powerful word was "agape" (pronounced "ah –gah-pay"). It is the kind of love that leaves us speechless because it is beyond all normal expectations, totally undeserved, without condition, unlimited in scope, unending in duration, and completely selfless.

Agape love is described as "long-suffering and kind, without envy or boastfulness, without arrogance or rudeness, never selfish, never hot-tempered, and never taking into account a wrong suffered." This kind of love overlooks the faults of others, always hopes for the best, encourages, trusts, forgives, endures, and never gives up. And it is not "feeling..." it is action.

I once knew a man who was an unfaithful husband of a remarkably loving wife. Some well-meaning friends decided to tell her what her husband was really like. They met with her and told her what everyone else but she seemed to know.

This amazing lady, upon hearing this, said, "I'm sorry, but you just don't know my husband. He loves me, and he would never do this! You have made a terrible mistake. It must be someone else. My husband is a good man. I know him. He would *never* do anything like that!"

When the man heard what his wife had said, it broke his heart. He couldn't continue to betray such trust and respect. Looking in the mirror, he vowed to become the kind of man his wife believed him to be.

We may be a long way from being as loving as the three "heroes" of these stories. But they were just ordinary people.

One who was ready to die if his sister could live.

One who was ready to learn to kiss the crooked mouth of his wife without her ever being made to feel ugly.

One who was determined to believe the best about someone in spite of all other opinions.

These people were not miracle workers or perfect people or great saints. They only did what you or I or anybody else could do if we only will. They had simply cared more for someone else than they did for themselves. Scripture says that it all starts with simple kindness.

Glen Campbell told it pretty well when he sang, *"If you'll try a little kindness, then you'll overlook the blindness of the narrow-minded people on the narrow-minded streets!"*

Let's start now. See who can be first to "blow somebody away" with a radical act of love!

46

When Things Go Wrong

*"Whatever they show you on television, folks,
the real God cannot be manipulated, and doesn't
want us to be!"*

Things were going smoothly, for the most part, as I approached the weekend, but all of that changed on a Sunday night when my brother Jeff called.

He was choking back tears as he told me that our youngest brother Joe had been found off the side of the road, lying unconscious and bleeding in a ditch, underneath his motorcycle. They had taken him to a hospital emergency room. Jeff's words devastated me as he related, "They aren't able to wake him up."

My immediate reaction was very emotional and sorrowful to the point of heartbreak. Falling onto the floor and burying my face into a recliner, I wailed loudly, cried bitterly, and desperately prayed with all the strength I had. I remember being so overwhelmed that I was oblivious to my surroundings and un-inhibited in showing my sorrow. My brother Joe is one of my favorite human beings, and I was not prepared to lose him.

Then, before the week was over, more bad things happened.

My elderly mother was hospitalized. Then, on Saturday, I got on my bicycle to go up to the park and run and play with my sweet black lab, Maggie. Maggie became a little too anxious to get there and ran out in front of a car and was hit.

Also, my taxes were due and I had caught a bad cold.

You've heard that "When it rains, it pours," and that was the certainly the case with me. It didn't take long for my personal situation in life to go from "pretty good" to "really bad!"

We all face stressful times in life, times of tragedy or terrible difficulty. Many times along the way we come face to face with our own helplessness. If I'm going to have problems, I would like to have them scheduled to arrive one at a time, with breaks in between, please! So far it has not worked out that way.

But concerning pain and problems, I think that I have gained some insight over the years. I hope that when you go through your own hard times you will remember some of them:

One thing to remember is that helplessness is not hope-lessness. Just as things get bad, they can and probably will get better again. Some of these things are not caused by us, are not our fault, and can't be fixed by us. But we can keep our determination, fix our attitude, and roll with the punches. I hope that doesn't sound like a cliché. All I am saying is that resilience is a quality we all must develop.

Please also try to avoid asking "Why?" If we find ourselves demanding to know the reason why something happened, we are putting ourselves in a higher position than we really occupy. We are not in charge, and we will not be given all the answers we want. You and I will just have to deal with that. If we don't, then our attitude compounds the problem. Plan and pray for a smooth road in life all you want, but it's not always going to happen. Looking for somebody to blame... demanding a solution or an explanation... it's all a symptom of our own arrogance.

If this sounds negative, it is not meant to be. It's just that if we don't willingly surrender our stubborn demands, we make everything much worse. The book of Job makes it clear. There is only one who understands and controls it all, and He doesn't usually ask for my advice!

He has gently reminded me that I'm not in management; I can only assist in the advertising department, and I don't do too well in that!

If you have a tendency to think that things would have turned out better "if only..." please understand that this is a popular way of wallowing in regret while trying to assess blame. It will get you nowhere.

I am sorry to even have to bring up this next pitfall, but some of the most sincere Christians are sometimes influenced by really bizarre theology. This theology throws out the Biblical teachings about perseverance and patience and endurance, and only emphasizes what they call "faith." This arrogant and unbalanced teaching proclaims that if you have a strong enough faith, you will always get an immediate, sensational, miraculous answer.

But whatever they may show you on television, folks, the real God cannot be manipulated and doesn't want us to be. The strongest faith is that which continues to trust, in spite of having no answers yet.

We all have a natural human tendency to run away from pain and heartbreak. We hate it. We can prevent some pain if we behave wisely, but hurts and sorrows will come to all of us. They are just a part of life in this world. Roses have thorns, bees have stingers, bugs bite, ants spoil your picnic, and birds eat your berries and then drop stuff on your head. This is all minor compared to what is done by husbands, wives, kids, neighbors, doctors, teachers, preachers, and the IRS, the CIA, and the HMOs.

When somebody is going through hard times, *please* spare the clichés and poems and even the Bible verses! They sound phony and hollow to the hurting soul.

Henri Nouwen said that trying to "fix" somebody instead of spending time suffering with them is merely another cruel form of rejection. I think he is right, and we need to learn to just be with the people we love, and share in their suffering... without artificially rushing them through it.

God doesn't always cooperate in our quest for an easy and comfortable existence, because He knows that hidden in the darkness and the pain from which we run we will find Him to be more real to us than ever before. The darker it is, the brighter the lantern shines. This is one of the great truths of life: that maturity and strength come as a result of adversity. Some call it "the school of hard knocks." For some of us it's the only school where we ever really learn.

I don't want this to sound trite. Sometimes the problems are overwhelming.

When it gets so bad that you don't think you can stand it, I hope that you will give yourself permission to be human! It's okay to cry out in protest, to complain, and even to get mad at God for a while. He can take it, and doesn't get angry when our sincere human emotions are being expressed.

Sometimes "cussin' and spittin'" is just part of being genuinely vulnerable. He is into earthy honesty... not pious pretense.

In conclusion, I need to let you know that things have turned out well for me in the recent difficulties I told you about! I am so thankful to report that Joe woke up and recovered! Mom came home and got well, and Maggie is fine except for a broken foot! I am okay, and the taxes are done, too. Sometimes we *do* get the good breaks and the happy endings!

But not always. Other things have happened in my life and in yours that didn't turn out so well. Rest assured that when the answers don't come as we wish... well, something within us is being built that takes a little longer.

The finished product will be worth the wait.

47

Who Really Touches Our Lives?

"It's not about being number one. It's about being a friend."

Someone sent me an e-mail that was a simple quiz, asking me if I could name the richest people in the world. Then it asked me to name the last three Heisman Trophy winners. Then the winners of the Super Bowl, the World Series, the Miss America contest, the Nobel Prize, and the Academy Awards. I got some of them right for this year, but didn't do well at all beyond that.

The headliners of yesterday, the best in their fields that achieved first place are soon forgotten, as are the also-rans and runners-up and honorable-mentions. The remembrance of all of these once-famous winners so quickly fades into oblivion. It doesn't take very long for the awards to tarnish, the certificates to fade, and for the applause and cheering to die.

Then there was a part two to the quiz. It asked me to remember a teacher who helped me along the way, a few friends who assisted in difficult times, a neighbor who did something special, an employer and an employee who went the extra mile, and somebody who made me feel special.

That second part was much easier. In fact, my mind began to think back to people who have long since gone out of my life, but who made a lasting impact.

There was a lady who invited me to a "Good News Club." I don't recall much about it, except that she used a flannelgraph, and she gave us cookies and told me that Jesus loved me so much He was willing to die for me. It was the best thing I had ever heard. I have no idea what the lady's name was, but fifty years later, what she taught is still good news for me.

I remember my second-grade teacher, Miss McInnis, who prayed for each one in her class... by name... out loud... every day. They would fire her for doing that today, but I suspect she would have done it anyway!

I remember a friend who took me with him when I was so shy, and introduced me to all of his friends, and some of those friends actually liked me, and suddenly the dirty air of Birmingham smelled like "home," and I loved it!

There was a lady whom I didn't even know who thought that my voice was so special she insisted that I sing two songs at her wedding though I had never done a solo before. But because she believed that I could do it, I practiced really hard and pulled it off!

I also remember a teacher in high school who thought one of my essays was so good that she read it to the whole class.

And there was this really beautiful girl in school who smiled at me and told me that she thought I was "cute." (It was a long time ago!)

And there were some strange but wonderful people who always laughed aloud at my jokes, even the dumb ones, saying I just "cracked them up."

Even that YMCA football game when my teammates cheered because I had sacked the opposing quarterback. I wasn't very good at football, but on that one play, that one time, I was great!

Then there was a lonely evening when I was discouraged and miserable, and an old friend from the distant past called me "out of the blue," inviting me to something that was being planned, saying it would not be the same without me.

And the time when I was leaving home for the day and my little boy started to cry. I promised to bring him back a little present, but he told me that he didn't want me to buy him anything. He said, "I don't want anything but to be with you."

And that cold November night when I thought that I would bring encouragement to my dying father by watching a football game with him on TV. In the first quarter, he said, "Jimmy, can you please turn off the ball game and just talk to me about my true home that I'm about to go to?"

And then there was that special and ecstatic time when the love of my life first looked at me and said, "I love you."

And the time many years later, when our hearts were broken and we had thought the marriage would end, that she sent me a card that simply said, "Come get me."

As I looked again at the quiz, I realized that none of the "top achievers" in any field had made any difference in my life at all. No World Series champion had been my friend. No Heisman Trophy winner had ever called me on the phone. No movie star had ever talked to me or prayed for me. But so many relatively unknown people had made enormous contributions to everything that is good in my life.

I realized that shiny trophies, coveted Oscars, and prestigious awards are fine for only a very short while. But those who invest in the lives of others are the real winners, the real heroes, the ones who will not be forgotten. It's not about success or fame or being in the record books. It's not about being number one. It's about being a friend. It doesn't take any special talent, but it takes time... and heart... and unselfishness... and caring enough to show up.

From a desperate and confusing time in the late sixties, the importance of being a friend came home to us meaningfully in a song by Simon and Garfunkel:

When you're weary — feeling small

When tears are in your eyes — I will dry them all;

I'm on your side when times get rough

And friends just can't be found,

Like a bridge over troubled water, I will lay me down.

Like a bridge over troubled water, I will lay me down.

Come to think of it, maybe that is a special talent — a very special one. I'm going to have to deal with the fact that I will never get an Oscar. I will never wear a World Series ring. I will never score a touchdown in a stadium. My name will not be engraved on a trophy.

But I can be a bridge over troubled waters for somebody who might not make it without me. Just like so many who helped me along the way, I couldn't have made it without them.

I will lay me down.

48

You Are Invited

"No riddles, no parables, no mystery. It is put into the form of a simple invitation."

The man was in prison and knew that he probably would never get out. He was tired and discouraged. He had done nothing wrong, and he had spent his entire life in one cause.

He even saw himself as a small part of a fulfillment of prophecy, as a voice crying in the wilderness. The message he had lived and preached all of his life was all about one thing... about a man who was to come after him... who would be the fulfillment of the best desires of all people.

He was what everyone would call an eccentric. He dressed differently. He ate differently. He lived differently. People had come to be baptized in a muddy river by him, and had he not spent a lot of time in that river he probably would have smelled pretty bad. His political incorrectness kept him in trouble, to say the least.

But now, after preaching to so many that the Messiah was coming after him, and after he had actually baptized this Messiah, and pointed him out to others as "the Lamb of God who takes away sins," then he himself... locked in that horrible prison and sitting on death row... this man that we have learned to call John the Baptist... began to doubt.

The message was sent through the agency of his friends on the outside. One stark and simple question, quickly passed along to the disciples of Jesus, until Jesus himself was confronted with the question. "Are you really the one? Are you the promised Messiah that we have waited for? Or shall we look for someone else?"

The message sent back was (as is so typical of Jesus) neither a yes or a no. It was, "Tell John what you are seeing! Tell him what you are hearing! Blind people can now see. Lame people are now walking. Lepers are cleansed. Dead people are raised up. Good news is being proclaimed to the lowly and poor. How happy will be the person who does not get offended at what I am doing, or how I am doing it!"

We are not told anything more about how the message was received. Was it enough? Was it the needed encouragement and reassurance? I can't help but think that it was. I want to believe that John received the message, understood it, and rejoiced in it until his death. But we are not told about that. We aren't even told that he got the message at all.

What we are told is that Jesus immediately gave honor to this man John, saying that he was indeed the fulfillment of prophecy, that he was "more than just a prophet," and that no woman had ever given birth to one who was greater than he was.

It's so remarkable to me that God always shows us how

our priorities and perceptions and presumptions are so off-target from His. When He said, "My thoughts are not your thoughts, and my ways are not your ways," it was a classic understatement! I may have degrees in the subject of theology, but, still, I often just don't "get it." So many things about God are beyond our understanding... mysterious... even unknowable.

But what amazes me most is that, before this day ends, and before this chapter (Matthew eleven) ends, the very most important message for us... the one we need the most... is put into the simplest, most unmistakable language possible. No riddles, no parables, no mystery. It is put into the form of a simple invitation:

"Come unto me, all of you who are weary and heavy-laden, and I will give you rest."

Here it is clearly told to us that, personally, I am invited. And you are invited. We know all about being weary and heavy-laden. We are heavy-laden with guilt over our own failures, but we are invited to come. The invitation is to all of us who are lonely and lost and laboring under the burden, those of us who have tried and failed and those who never really tried at all. The invited are you and me, and all of us who honestly see ourselves as unworthy and unable and unqualified or disqualified. Those invited include the desiring, the despairing, the distressed, the depressed, the destroyed, the damned, the doomed, and the dying. They are you and me, our family and neighbors and friends and enemies. They are the black and the white, the rich and the poor, the known and the unknown, who are battered, bleeding and bruised, bitter and broken, burned out and burdened with sin. They are those who were abused and betrayed by religion and by religious people, and who learned to do the same to others. They are we... the scared and the scarred and the shamed and the suffering, the hapless and hopeless and helpless, the wounded and weary and worn-out, the tired and the tried, the troubled and torn. The ones who yielded to temptation. The ones who went to the wrong places to fulfill their desires. The ones who went away and couldn't find their way back... who went too far, paid too much, and stayed too long. It is to all of us... and to each of us... that Jesus simply says, "Come unto me."

"Come with your shame and your sorrow and your sin, but come. Come with your remorse and your regrets, your doubts and your dilemmas, but come.

"Come... my arms are open.

"Come... my eyes are full of forgiveness and compassion.

"Come... I am not angry with you.

"Come... I understand. It will be okay. We will work it out.

"Come... not just once, but many times, whether your troubles be many or few, whether great or small.

"You will learn that I am gentle and meek and lowly and humble of heart. I have no desire to punish you, rebuke you, embarrass you or reject you.

"My yoke is easy. My burden is light. You don't have to pay anything... it is already paid for. You don't have to do anything... it is already done. I am crucified and risen. It is finished. I loved you that much.

"Come unto me!"

Jim Lee

Acknowledgements

I would like to thank all of the people who encouraged me to write : First to my daughter-in-law Teth, who started a magazine in 2004, and insisted that I put a "column" in each monthly issue, which I did for more than six years.

I want to thank the hundreds of people who called me or wrote me or stopped me on the streets of Fairhope, Alabama, saying they had liked what I wrote.

I want to thank those who helped me in the faith at a young age. There were so many, but I particularly want to mention Rev. Dick Thomassian, the youth minister in my home church, and the late Dr. Alden Gannett, who was president of the Bible College I attended.

I want to thank those who introduced me to a deeper understanding of grace, through their ministry and through their books. First among them is Steve Brown of Key Life ministries (ww.keylife.org) who also wrote a generous preface to this book. And the grace-filled authors who were able to break through my performance-oriented religion, particularly Brennan Manning, Philip Yancey, Frederick Buechner, Robert F. Capon, Larry Crabb, and Henri Nouwen.

Sometimes the names have been changed to protect the guilty, but I want to thank all of those who touched my life in such a way that I wanted to write about you. These stories are your stories as well as mine

Many thanks to Cheryl Sturdy for helping me get the original manuscript together.

Thanks also to Fred and Blair Garth and to all the helpers and workers at Lost Key Publishing who helped me to finally make a book out of it.

And to you who now have this in your hands... my biggest thanks of all.

Especially if you paid for it!

IF YOU REALLY LIKE THIS BOOK, and...

If you would you like more copies of "Broken Roads to Grace" …

Or if you would like to order the two-CD audio book of "Broken Roads to Grace"…

Or if you want to order several copies at a discounted price…

Or if you want to follow Jim Lee's weekly blog…

Or if you want info on Jim Lee's next book …

Then please go online to:
www.brokenroadstograce.com

Email Jim Lee at:
jim@brokenroadstograce.com

Or order by mail from:

P U B L I S H I N G
7166 SHARP REEF
PERDIDO KEY, FL 32507

Shameless Self-promotion Page

Jim Lee

If you are helped by the message of "Broken Roads to Grace," please help me to spread the word however you are able.

If you have a website, a blog, or a Facebook or Twitter account, say some nice things about it and link to **www.brokenroadstograce.com**.

If you decide to invite me to speak at your event, I promise you this:

(1) I show up. (2) I show up on time. (3) I work cheap. (4) I am not a Prima Donna. (5) I promise not to play the accordion. (6) If I could sell a hundred books I would go anywhere this side of Idaho for a dollar and a half.

Please feel free to email me at **jim@brokenroadstograce.com** or call me at **(251) 510-7141**.